BY THE EDITORS OF CON

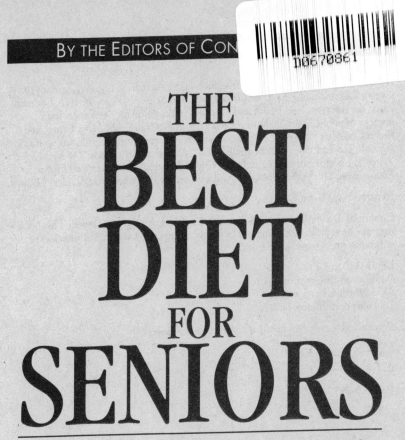

THE
BEST
DIET
FOR
SENIORS

How to find a weight-loss plan that fits

Densie Webb, Ph.D., R.D.

Publications International, Ltd.

Densie Webb, Ph.D., R.D., is a freelance writer and editor. She is the author of seven books, including *Foods for Better Health* and *Super Nutrition After 50*. For many years, she has translated health and nutrition information for consumers for a number of publications, including *Family Circle, Fitness, Parade, Men's Fitness,* and *Redbook*. She has been the health editor at *McCall's* magazine, a regular columnist for *Woman's Day* and *Prevention* magazine, and a regular contributor to *The New York Times*. She is currently a columnist for *GreatLife* magazine, associate editor for *Environmental Nutrition* newsletter, and a writer for the American Botanical Council.

Illustrations: Martin Côté

This book is for information purposes and is not intended to provide medical advice. Neither Publications International, Ltd., nor the author, editors, or publisher take responsibility for any possible consequences from any treatment, procedure, exercise, dietary modification, action, or application of medication or preparation by any person reading or following the information in this book. The publication of this book does not constitute the practice of medicine, and this book does not attempt to replace your physician or other health care provider. Before undertaking any course of treatment, the author, editors, and publisher advise the reader to check with a physician or other health care provider.

The brand name products mentioned in this publication are trademarks or service marks of their respective companies. The mention of any product in this publication does not constitute an endorsement by the respective proprietors of Publications International, Ltd., nor does it constitute an endorsement by any of these companies that their products should be used in the manner recommended by this publication.

Table of Contents

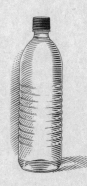

Introduction

If you want to lose weight, chances are that you're constantly searching for the ultimate diet— one that will let you eat what you want when you want it and still lose weight fast. While that may be asking a bit much, there

are plenty of diet plans and diet books that can help you safely and comfortably reach your goal. One of them is right for you. But which one?

Choosing a diet that will work for you, and one that can accommodate the changing nutrition needs of older adults, is a considerable challenge. Should you go with a high-protein diet or a sugar-free one? Food-combining and blood-typing diets sound interesting, but is there real science behind them? And what about celebrity diets or well-known diet programs like Dieting With the Duchess or Jenny Craig? The choices are plentiful, but impartial and expert information about how to pick a diet, especially one that's good for seniors, is rare.

That's where this book comes in. Its purpose is to help you evaluate some of

the most popular diet books and plans on the market and choose one that's healthy and fits your personality and lifestyle. That way, you'll have a diet plan you can stick with for good.

To help you assess the diets, the opening chapters give you a guided tour of healthful eating. Along the way, you'll learn just how important physical activity is to weight loss and some techniques for getting your calorie-burning engine revved up. We also provide a self-test that will help you evaluate any diet—not just the ones reviewed here—to see if it's right for you. The bulk of the book is devoted to reviews of 30 popular diet books and programs, giving you the particulars and the pros and cons of each.

Weight loss is all about choices—whether it's choosing a diet plan, a way to increase your physical activity, or a strategy for managing your food cravings. In this book, we give you the information you need to weigh all the options and make dieting choices you can live with.

Your Changing Nutrition Needs

As you age, your body requires more of some nutrients, such as B vitamins, and less of others, such as iron. But adapting to your changing needs isn't as simple as adjusting your nutritional intake up or down. That's because body changes cause you to become less efficient at utilizing some of the nutrients in the food you eat. You do need to know which nutrients to boost and which ones to cut back on, but you must also know how to make the most of dietary sources. This knowledge can mean the difference between maintaining your good health as you age and being vulnerable to life-threatening diseases, such as cancer, diabetes, and heart disease, or to life-altering changes such as memory loss and a decline in mental acuity.

This chapter will discuss how your nutritional needs change. The next chapter will guide you as you make food choices to meet these changing needs.

Vitamin Basics

Vitamins play an important role in virtually all the important events in the body, including the production of energy, hormones, enzymes, immune cells, and neurotransmitters (chemical messengers in the brain). Vitamins can be divided into two general categories: fat-soluble (A, D, E, and K) and water-soluble (the B's and C). It doesn't take much of any one vitamin to meet your needs. While proteins, carbohydrates, and fats are measured in grams, vitamins are measured in milligrams (one-thousandths of a gram) and micrograms (one-millionths of a gram). But those microscopic amounts have powerful health-promoting properties. Although we tend to think of supplements when we talk about vitamins, food—not supplements—should be your primary source. Fruits and vegetables are the primary sources of water-soluble vitamins and some fat-soluble vitamins (beta-carotene, which the body converts to A; E; and K). Fortified dairy products are the primary dietary source of vitamin D. Your skin also manufactures some vitamin D when exposed to sunlight, which explains its nickname: "the sunshine vitamin."

Vitamins That Increase in Importance as You Age

There are quite a lot of nutrients that you will need more of as you age but only a few that you will need less of. The following nutrients are those you need to get more of now that you're over 50:

Vitamin B2 (Riboflavin)
Recommended Intake
  Men: 1.3 milligrams a day
  Women: 1.1 milligrams a day

This B vitamin makes it possible for your body to access energy from the food you eat, and it helps each of the body's cells produce its own energy. It also plays an important role in maintaining your vision and keeping your skin healthy. Riboflavin is required for the production of niacin, another B vitamin. While the recommended intake for riboflavin doesn't actually increase with age, the fact that it stays the same while your calorie needs drop means that you have to make wise food choices to get enough riboflavin in your diet. Moreover, researchers suspect that you become more sensitive to riboflavin deficiencies with age.

Vitamin B6 (Pyridoxine)

Recommended Intake
   Men: 1.7 milligrams a day
   Women: 1.5 milligrams a day

Vitamin B6 helps new cells to develop and is an important participant in the production of the B vitamin niacin and the neurotransmitter serotonin. It boosts the immune system and helps to regulate blood sugar levels. Pyridoxine is also a member of the trio of B vitamins (B6, B12, folic acid) that help reduce your risk of heart disease by keeping blood levels of the amino acid homocysteine low. High levels of homocysteine have been linked with clogged arteries and heart disease.

As you age, your risk of developing a vitamin B6 deficiency increases. There are two reasons for that. First, older people generally consume less protein, which is the richest source of vitamin B6, so their diets are more likely to be low in it.

Second, many older adults metabolize the vitamin more rapidly than they did when they were younger, increasing the need for it on a daily basis. Signs of severe vitamin B6 deficiency include skin problems, anemia, depression, confusion, and convulsions.

Vitamin B12 (Cyanocobalamin/ cobalamin)

Recommended Intake
   Men: 2.4 micrograms a day
   Women: 2.4 micrograms a day

Vitamin B12 is critical for proper nerve and brain development and for the production of healthy red blood cells. If you don't get enough of this vitamin, mental functioning can diminish and balance and coordination can be impaired. A prolonged, severe deficiency of B12 that goes uncorrected can cause irreversible nerve damage.

A B12 deficiency usually is not caused by a lack of B12 in

the diet. The vitamin is found in animal foods such as meat and liver, as well as in eggs, fish, and dairy products. Only strict vegetarians who don't eat dairy or eggs are at risk of a deficiency because of diet. A B12 deficiency is usually the result of either pernicious anemia, an inherited disease in which the stomach lining stops producing a substance called intrinsic factor that is needed to absorb vitamin B12, or a lack of stomach acid, which is also fundamental to the absorption of the vitamin.

A decline in stomach acid, a condition called atrophic gastritis, is experienced by as many as 30 percent of people age 50 and older and by 40 percent of those age 80 and older. However, most do not realize they have the condition. Pernicious anemia also becomes much more common with age.

A deficiency caused by atrophic gastritis can be treated with vitamin B12 supplementation because the synthetic form doesn't require stomach acid. Pernicious anemia, however, must be treated with injections of vitamin B12.

In recent years, researchers have learned that, along with vitamins B6 and folic acid, B12 can also help ward off heart disease, stroke, and peripheral vascular disease by preventing the buildup of homocysteine, an artery-clogging compound that sometimes accumulates in the blood.

Folate/Folic acid
Recommended Intake
> *Men: 400 micrograms a day*
> *Women: 400 micrograms*
> *a day*

Folate is the catch-all term used to describe different forms of this B vitamin. However, folate refers to the forms found in food, while folic acid is the synthetic form found in vitamin supplements. This is the last of the B trio to tackle the buildup of homocysteine in the blood. It also appears to play an important role in keeping cells healthy and fending off potentially cancerous changes. Research has suggested that getting enough folate may help protect against cancers of the cervix, colon, and rectum. A low intake of folate may not, by itself, trigger cancerous changes in cells, but when combined with other potentially harmful cellular changes, it could be the final factor that causes cancer.

Folate is also needed for the production of proteins that build, maintain, and repair tissues—a process that continues throughout your life.

Choline

Recommended Intake
Men: 550 milligrams a day
Women: 425 milligrams a day

This is probably the least well-known of the "B's." It was officially recognized as an essential nutrient for the first time in 1998 and is involved in a wide variety of body functions. Choline is the raw material of neurotransmitters and cell membranes. Animal studies suggest that adequate intake of choline early in life can diminish the severity of memory loss that comes with aging. Recommended intakes are no higher for someone who is 69 than for someone who is 19. Some animal research suggests that choline may help improve memory in older adults, but human studies are needed to determine if choline is useful for preventing dementia in people as they age. It can be difficult to assess whether you are getting enough choline since it is not specifically listed on the Nutrition Facts label of food products.

Vitamin C

Recommended Intake
Men: 60 milligrams a day
Women: 60 milligrams a day

Another of the water-soluble vitamins, C is probably best

known for its purported role in fending off colds. While it may help reduce the duration and the severity of cold symptoms, it's never been proved to prevent the cold itself. It is, however, a proven antioxidant nutrient that helps to neutralize free radicals that can damage DNA. Damaged DNA can turn normal cells into cancerous ones. Vitamin C also plays a critical role in the formation of white blood cells that fight infection and in the production of collagen, the connective tissue that holds skin, bone, ligaments, and cartilage together. Vitamin C helps keep blood vessel walls strong and tiny blood vessels pliable and resistant to damage. If that's not enough, it also is essential to the production of red blood cells, plays a role in wound healing, and helps keep gums healthy.

Getting enough vitamin C is especially important as you get older because of its role in preventing diseases, especially those to which you are more susceptible as you age. Vitamin C helps fight heart disease by regulating cholesterol levels in the blood, fights free radicals that cause cataracts and macular degeneration, and helps protect against cancers of the esophagus, stomach, pancreas, cervix, rectum, breast, and lung.

Because smokers have lower blood levels of vitamin C than nonsmokers, the recommended intake for smokers is 100 milligrams a day. However, some vitamin C experts say that to get optimum protection, it may be best for everyone to saturate the body's tissues with the nutrient, which takes as much as 200 milligrams a day.

Vitamin D

Recommended Intake
  Men and Women over 50:
    400 International Units a day
  Men and Women over 70:
    600 International Units a day

Almost all the calcium in your body is stored in your

bones, and vitamin D plays a critical role in making sure it gets there. The vitamin acts as calcium's gatekeeper, regulating the absorption of this essential mineral. Vitamin D helps keep bones strong and helps maintain blood levels of calcium so it can be used as needed for other body functions, such as muscle contractions and the transmission of nerve impulses.

Some vitamin D is produced in your skin when it is exposed to the sun. The ultraviolet rays of the sun act as a trigger for conversion to an active form. In healthy people, it takes only about 10 to 15 minutes of unprotected exposure to the sun on a summer day to make enough vitamin D to store in the liver, a reserve that can last for months. However, if you're slathering on sunscreen—as you should to prevent skin cancer—you may not be getting enough sunlight for the conversion to take place. The best advice is to get a few minutes of unprotected sun exposure in the early morning or late afternoon, when the sun's rays are least likely to damage your skin.

As you age, the recommended intake of this fat-soluble vitamin increases more than for any other nutrient.

Why the jump? As your skin ages, it loses some of its ability to produce vitamin D when it is exposed to sunlight. To make matters worse, the body doesn't absorb vitamin D from the diet as well as it did when you were younger. Inadequate vitamin D can translate into weak bones, osteoporosis, and bone fractures. Getting enough vitamin D is especially important for menopausal and postmenopausal women to help slow the rapid rate of bone loss that typically occurs.

Vitamin E

Recommended Intake
   *Men: 10 International Units
   a day*
   *Women: 10 International
   Units a day*

Another of the fat-soluble vitamins, vitamin E acts as an antioxidant, protecting the body's cells from free radicals, a destructive form of oxygen that damages DNA and can turn normal cells into cancerous ones. The recommended intake for vitamin E doesn't increase with age, but dietary surveys show that more than 50 percent of men and more than 75 percent of women over the age of 51 don't get the recommended intake. And some researchers believe that much higher intakes of E— around 200 to 400 International Units (IU) a day—may help lower the risk of heart disease, cataracts, and prostate cancer. Though recent studies have called into question E's effectiveness in holding heart disease at bay, 200 to 400 IU of E a day is still a healthy idea.

Vitamin K

Recommended Intake
   Men: 120 micrograms a day
   Women: 90 micrograms a day

Vitamin K is one of the less glamorous vitamins, long known mainly for its role in blood clotting. But this fat-soluble vitamin also plays an important role in bone metabolism, which is just beginning to be understood. The recommended intake doesn't increase with age, but the recommended intakes for men and women of all ages were recently raised in light of new findings showing the potential role of vitamin K in health. And dietary surveys show that half of men and women over the age of 51 don't get the current recommended intake of the vitamin. Research has shown that people with osteo-porosis and bone fractures have lowered blood levels of vitamin K. It's believed that vitamin K is important for activating the bone-building protein osteocalcin. If there is not enough vitamin K to acti-vate this important protein, then osteoporosis can result. Vitamin K may also help pre-vent arteries from becoming clogged; researchers are cur-rently investigating this.

Mineral Basics

The minerals needed to keep your body functioning far outnumber the vitamins. In fact, it's estimated there are more than 60 minerals in your body. Although recommended intakes have been set for only 17, researchers are on the verge of declaring a few more minerals essential to good health. Though we don't hear about minerals (with the notable exceptions of calcium iron, and sodium) as much as we do vitamins, minerals are

just as critical to good health. They are essential for building bones and teeth, keeping your heart beating regularly, and helping your blood to clot. Like vitamins, minerals can be divided into two groups: macrominerals (macro means large) such as calcium, phos-phorus, potassium, and sodium, which are required in relatively large amounts, and trace minerals such as boron, chromium, copper, fluoride, iodine, iron, manganese, molybdenum, selenium, and zinc, which are required in small amounts.

Minerals That Increase in Importance as You Age

Calcium
Recommended Intake
   Men: 1,200 milligrams a day
   Women: 1,200 milligrams a day

There has been a lot of research on calcium, and much

has been written about it. But there's still not 100 percent agreement on how much calcium we need to keep our bones strong as we age. The official 1997 recommendation from the Food and Nutrition Board is given on the previous page. But prior to that, in 1994, the National Institutes of Health had issued the following recommendations: 1,000 milligrams a day for men aged 50 to 65 and women of the same age who are taking estrogen replacement therapy and 1,500 milligrams for women age 50 to 65 who are not taking estrogen replacement and all men and women older than 65. Regardless of which recommendation is right, the fact remains that most of us don't get nearly enough of this bone-building mineral. Dietary surveys show that 90 percent of women ages 19 to 70 don't get enough. Overall, most American adults consume less than half of the amount recommended by the Food and Nutrition Board. A low calcium intake, coupled with inadequate production of vitamin D, greatly increases the risk of bone fractures in older people. Getting enough calcium and vitamin D every day can decrease the risk.

An adequate intake of calcium also may contribute to the taming of high blood pressure and the prevention of polyps in the colon (growths in the colon that sometimes turn cancerous).

Magnesium

Recommended Intake
> *Men: 420 milligrams a day*
> *Women: 320 milligrams a day*

Like calcium and vitamin D, magnesium is an essential nutrient for bone health. However, its importance in the body is much more far-reaching. Proof of that is the fact that magnesium is involved in more than 300 metabolic processes in the body, including muscle contraction, protein synthesis, cell reproduction, energy metabolism, and the transport of nutrients into cells. It often acts as a trigger for these processes. Magnesium is most studied, however, for its role in bone health, blood pressure regulation, cardiovascular health, and diabetes. Several studies have found that elderly people get little magnesium in their diets. That, combined with the fact that, with age, magnesium absorption decreases and excretion in urine increases, provides the perfect formula for magnesium depletion and deficiency.

Potassium
Recommended Intake
   None established

Though there is no official recommended intake set for this mineral, experts have estimated that you need between 1,600 and 2,000 milligrams a day—more if you have high blood pressure. That's because potassium is intimately involved in regulating blood pressure. In fact, the Food and Drug Administration recently approved a health claim for foods rich in potassium that says, "Diets containing foods that are good sources of potassium and low in sodium may reduce the risk of high blood pressure and stroke." Potassium is present in all the cells in your body and plays a vital role in muscle contraction, transmission of nerve impulses, and maintenance of fluid balance. While we don't know if the need for potassium increases with age, we do know that the risk of high blood pressure does, making it even more important to get plenty of potassium in your diet. Ironically, many medications that are prescribed to treat high blood pressure actually drain the body of potassium, increasing the need for the mineral even more.

Selenium
Recommended Intake
 Men: 55 micrograms a day
 Women: 55 micrograms a day

Selenium is another anti-oxidant miracle worker, helping to protect against cancers of the colon, prostate, and lungs while boosting your immune system. Because the risk of cancer increases with age, it's important to get enough selenium to minimize your risk. Selenium works in two major ways to fend off the disease-causing damage of free radicals. It works side by side with vitamin E, sparing the vitamin while it shares the antioxidant burden. It also is needed for the production of an enzyme called glutathione peroxidase, which is a key player in the body's sophisticated defense system. Because selenium is easily absorbed, it's also easy to

take too much. Experts recommend that you not get more than 400 micrograms a day.

Chromium
Recommended Intake
 Men: 30 micrograms a day
 Women: 20 micrograms a day

Chromium stimulates the action of insulin, the hormone that helps blood sugar gain entry into the cells. The mineral is also needed for the body to properly metabolize fat and to keep blood levels of cholesterol and triglycerides in check. As you age, chromium levels in the body drop and insulin resistance increases, resulting in high blood sugar levels, which makes chromium a mineral to watch in your diet. Unfortunately, there are some obstacles to getting adequate chromium, and researchers now recognize that older people may be more vulnerable to chromium depletion. First of all, eating a lot of refined carbohydrates, such as those found in candy, cookies, cakes, and soft drinks, depletes your body's chromium stores. If you're a fan of sweets, you'll need to change your ways to ensure you're making the most of the chromium in your diet. Secondly, a decrease in chromium stores seems to occur with age. Finally, some medications may cause a depletion of chromium. All these factors combined make it difficult to maintain an adequate level of chromium in the body.

Zinc

Recommended Intake
   Men: 11 milligrams a day
   Women: 9 milligrams a day

Zinc is one busy mineral! Not only is it involved in the metabolism of carbohydrates, fat, and protein, it also plays an important role in the production of DNA, the blueprint for every cell in the body. And it's a part of the structure of insulin, making it crucial for regulating blood sugar levels.

To round out its résumé, zinc also is essential for wound healing and for maintaining your immunity and your sense of taste as you age. Dietary surveys show that about 50 percent of men and 75 percent of women over the age of 51 don't get enough zinc in their diets, making supplementation a good idea. And while a high-fiber diet is good for your health, it can interfere with your body's ability to absorb the zinc in your diet. But, if you take in too much zinc, you can actually suppress your body's ability to fight infection and negatively affect your sense of taste. While it's critical that you get the recommended intake of zinc every day, experts recommend not taking in more than 60 milligrams a day because it may interfere with copper absorption, immune function, and taste.

Other Nutrients That Increase in Importance as You Age

Protein

Recommended Intake
  Men: 63 grams a day
  Women: 50 grams a day

You need protein because your body requires the individual amino acids that link together to form proteins in foods. Once you eat protein-containing foods, the proteins are separated into individual amino acids in your digestive system and are used to build, repair, and maintain your body's tissues (skin, muscles, internal organs). Though they can be assembled in an almost infinite number of combinations, there are only 20 amino acids. Nine are essential, meaning they must come from your diet. Your body can manufacture the rest. Foods that contain all nine essential amino acids, such as fish, poultry, eggs, milk, and beef, are called "complete proteins." All protein provides four calories per gram and can be used for energy by the body if carbohydrates and fat are in short supply, as they are in some types of weight-loss diets.

Some experts believe that the current recommended intakes for folks over 50 fall short of what they really need. As you get older, your body becomes less and less efficient at processing the protein you take in, and your body is less able to hold onto protein stores. For seniors who are physically active, that goes double, since protein is needed to maintain muscle mass. But don't opt for protein shakes, powders, and bars. If you suffer from liver or kidney disease, you could be doing more harm than good since too much protein can stress your organs. You can get all the protein you need by making wise dietary choices.

Fluid

While you may not think of it this way, water is a vital nutrient. You may be able to survive for weeks without food, but the body can last only a few days without water. Water has a ubiquitous presence in the body and is involved in virtually every metabolic process: the digestion of food, the absorption of nutrients, the circulation of the blood, the maintenance of proper body temperature, the cushioning of joints and organs, and the elimination of toxic metabolic byproducts from the body. When your body loses too much water through perspiration, vomiting, or excessive urination, or when you simply do not consume enough water, you become dehydrated. And dehydration is the most frequent reason people over the age of 65 are hospitalized. Half of the water in your body is lost from your lungs when you breathe (that's why your breath is moist) and from your skin through perspiration. Even if you don't feel like you're sweating, you are constantly losing some fluid through your skin. The Tufts University food pyramid for older Americans recommends that people over 70 drink eight 8-ounce glasses of water, juice, or milk every day. Even if you're only 50, it could do your body good. Hot temperatures and high altitude further increase your fluid needs. Why the emphasis on fluids for those over 50? As you age, your kidneys are less able to hold onto water, leaving you more vulnerable to dehydration. A low fluid intake can contribute to constipation, and recent research has found a link between inadequate fluid intake and kidney stones and bladder cancer.

Nutrients That Decrease in Importance as You Age

While there are fewer nutrients that fall into this category, it's important to know which ones they are because getting too much of these can be just as bad for you as not getting enough of the ones you need more of.

Vitamin A

Recommended Intake
  Men: 3,000 International
    Units a day
  Women: 2,300 International
    Units a day

Vitamin A, also known as retinol, has the distinction of being the only vitamin that you should consume less of as you get older. That's because you're able to store vitamin A more efficiently as you age and you metabolize it at a slower rate. That translates into higher levels of vitamin A in the blood. An important player in good health, vitamin A is essential for normal vision, gene expression, tissue growth, and proper immune function. But if you take in too much, you could be hurting your bones. Research has shown that men and women age 51 and older who take in too much vitamin A are at an increased risk of hip fracture, a risk that's over and above the increased risk that typically occurs with age. Going overboard with vitamin A (25,000 IU a day for an extended period of time) is toxic to your liver. Headaches, vomiting, and hair loss could be signs you're getting too much. A safer way to meet your vitamin A needs is through carotenoids, related plant-based materials that the body converts to vitamin A as needed.

Iron

Recommended Intake
  Men: 8 milligrams a day
  Women: 8 milligrams a day

Iron is best known for its role in the formation of healthy red blood cells, which are responsible for carrying oxygen through the blood. Iron is also a component of myoglobin, the compound that stores oxygen in muscle tissues. Oxygen is, of course, essential for life, and without iron to keep those red blood cells coming, you would die. But iron also has an important job in bolstering the immune system, helping the body to convert beta-carotene to vitamin A and to manufacture amino acids. There are two types of iron, heme and nonheme. Heme iron is found in meat, while nonheme iron is found in plants. Nonheme iron is less well absorbed, but that can be easily remedied by eating a food rich in vitamin C with a food rich in nonheme iron, since vitamin C aids in its absorption. While iron remains an essential nutrient, as you age your body needs less of the mineral. That's especially true of women after menopause. The risk of continuing to bolster your iron intake as you pass 50 is that you could unknowingly be suffering from a condition known as hemochromatosis. Also known as iron overload, hemochromatosis occurs when the body gets saturated with iron and isn't able to discard the extra. Untreated, it has the potential to harm every organ in your body. Some experts say it is the most common genetic disorder in the country. It is most common among Caucasians of northern European ancestry. Symptoms can include chronic fatigue and persistent aches and pains in your joints.

Sodium

Recommended Intake
  Men: a maximum of 2,400 milligrams a day
  Women: a maximum of 2,400 milligrams a day

Though the maximum recommended intake for this mineral set by many experts is 2,400 milligrams a day, the body actually requires only about 50 milligrams a day. But sodium is present in nearly all foods. Processed foods are especially high in sodium, making it easy to overdo. Get too much sodium and you could aggravate high blood pressure, which increases your risk of heart attack and stroke. Not everyone is sensitive to sodium's effects on blood pressure, but there is no way to identify those who are sodium-sensitive. In addition, a high-sodium diet can cause your body to lose calcium, increasing your risk for osteoporosis. As a result, experts generally recommend that everyone watch their sodium intake.

Calories

Recommended Intake
  Men, lightly to moderately active: about 2,300 calories a day
  Women, lightly to moderately active: about 1,900 calories a day

Calories are the energy your body extracts from the carbo-hydrates, proteins, and fats in the food you eat. You need a certain number of calories for your body to function. You'll need more calories if you're physically active, less if you're more of a couch potato. Men generally need more calories than women, and young people require more calories than older people. If you're 50+ and not physically active, you really have to keep an eye on your calorie intake or you could put on pounds that put you at risk for heart disease, diabetes, and some kinds of cancer. The key is to make every calorie count. Since your need for many nutrients increases with age, you can make every calorie count by choosing low-calorie foods that are brimming with nutrients. Here's a sobering thought: It takes only 100 extra calories a day to end up with an extra 10 pounds on your frame at the end of a year. You would either have to become more active or eat less to undo the damage.

The Best Ways to Meet Your Changing Nutrition Needs

Because you need fewer calories as you get older, your food choices are more critical than ever. You've got only so many calories with which to make the right decisions. If you don't choose wisely, you may gain weight while attempting to pack all your nutritional needs into your daily diet—and weight gain carries its own set of health risks.

To help older people manage nutritional and caloric intake, the Human Nutrition Research Center on Aging at Tufts University developed a food guide pyramid specifically for people age 70 and older. (See page 25.) The pyramid's recommendations speak directly to the age-related body changes that result in the need for specific nutrients and fluid. It's a good guide, too, for anyone over age 50.

Whether you're trying to lose weight, stay fit, or just feel better, it's important to pack the most nutritious foods possible into your daily diet. In the following pages we'll explain how to pick the foods that give you the biggest nutritional "bang" for the least caloric "buck."

Protein

The majority of foods contain at least some protein. Foods from animals, such as milk, eggs, beef, poultry, and fish, are highest in protein. Fruits, vegetables, and grains provide less. Getting enough protein usually is not a problem. In fact, most of us get more protein than we need. One serving of meat (about the size of a deck of cards), poultry, or fish provides about 50 percent of your daily protein requirement.

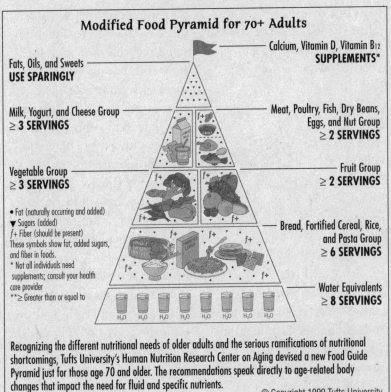

Modified Food Pyramid for 70+ Adults

Calcium, Vitamin D, Vitamin B12
SUPPLEMENTS*

Fats, Oils, and Sweets
USE SPARINGLY

Milk, Yogurt, and Cheese Group
≥ 3 SERVINGS

Meat, Poultry, Fish, Dry Beans,
Eggs, and Nut Group
≥ 2 SERVINGS

Vegetable Group
≥ 3 SERVINGS

Fruit Group
≥ 2 SERVINGS

• Fat (naturally occurring and added)
▼ Sugars (added)
f+ Fiber (should be present)
These symbols show fat, added sugars,
and fiber in foods.
* Not all individuals need
supplements; consult your health
care provider
**≥ Greater than or equal to

Bread, Fortified Cereal, Rice,
and Pasta Group
≥ 6 SERVINGS

Water Equivalents
≥ 8 SERVINGS

Recognizing the different nutritional needs of older adults and the serious ramifications of nutritional shortcomings, Tufts University's Human Nutrition Research Center on Aging devised a new Food Guide Pyramid just for those age 70 and older. The recommendations speak directly to age-related body changes that impact the need for fluid and specific nutrients.

What about protein supplements? They may seem like a quick protein fix, but most nutritionists say they offer few benefits. Protein supplements can be costly, both to your pocketbook and your waistline, since they're expensive and high in calories. And you have to be careful not to overload on protein or you could tax your kidneys, the organs responsible for discarding waste once protein has been digested. That can happen if you add a protein supplement to a diet that's already plentiful in protein.

Protein Power

Below is a list of concentrated sources of animal protein. Choose low fat varieties.

Beef
Chicken
Eggs
Fish
Milk
Pork
Tofu
Turkey
Yogurt

Fat

You may be accustomed to hearing that fat is bad, but the truth is you need some fat in your diet to stay healthy. Fat carries the fat-soluble vitamins A, D, E, and K and components of fat known as essential fatty acids. There are three major types of fatty acids: saturated, which are found mainly in animal foods; monounsaturated, which are found mainly in plant foods, such as olive oil; and polyunsaturated fats, also found in plant foods and in fish. The amount of fat you need—about 20 to 30 percent of your day's calorie intake—stays pretty much the same regardless of your age. However, because fat has the most concentrated calorie count (nine calories per gram), you'll need to control your fat intake. Otherwise you could put on unwanted pounds.

The flip side of that, however, is not to go too low. Extremely low fat diets (ten percent of calories or less) can deprive your body of the essential fatty acids and fat-soluble vitamins it needs.

Choosing the right kind of fat is the key to staying healthy while managing your calorie intake. Focus on getting fewer saturated fats, which clog the arteries, and more of monounsaturated and polyunsaturated fats to keep your arteries clean and your heart healthy. If you can, try to stick primarily with monounsaturated fats. And make sure that some of the polyunsaturated fats in your diet come from fish and flaxseed. Research suggests that these fats may help reduce dangerous blood clotting, prevent abnormal heart rhythms, improve immune function, keep your eyes healthy and your brain functioning properly, fight depression, ease the pain of arthritis, and possibly even reduce the risk of breast cancer.

Foods High in Saturated Fat
Butter
Cheese
Cream
Fatty cuts of meat
Ground turkey
Ice cream
Whole milk

Foods High in Monounsaturated Fat
Avocado
Canola oil
Olive oil
Walnuts

Foods High in Polyunsaturated Fat
Corn oil
Fish (anchovies, bass, herring, mackerel, salmon, trout, tuna)
Flaxseed
Safflower oil
Sesame oil
Soybean oil
Sunflower oil

Carbohydrates

Carbohydrates are your best source for instant energy, B vitamins, and fiber—if you choose whole grains. Current recommendations, no matter your age, are to get 55 to 60 percent of your day's calories from carbohydrates. Most of that should come from fruits, vegetables, and whole grains. There's little room in a healthful diet for sugar and other refined carbohydrates, such as white bread, when you're trying to get the most nutrients you can for the fewest calories. Make sure you keep tabs on the "extras" that traditionally go hand-in-hand with carbohydrates, such as margarine, cream cheese, cheese, and cream sauces. These high-calorie, high fat add-ons can turn even healthful carbohydrate foods into dietary disasters. Carbohydrates, by themselves, provide four calories per gram.

A Collection of High-Carbohydrate Foods

Bran flakes
Brown rice
Canned or dried
    beans and
    peas
Dried fruit
Lentils
Popcorn
Shredded wheat
Tortilla chips, baked
Whole-wheat pastas

Fiber

Fiber, a form of carbohydrate, helps prevent constipation and maintain a healthy balance of "good" bacteria in your intestinal tract. There are two types of fiber, each with its particular benefits. Soluble fiber forms a gel in the intestinal tract that carries unwanted cholesterol out of the body. It can also help regulate blood sugar levels. Insoluble fiber is known for its ability to help prevent and treat constipation. Strive for 20 to 35 grams of fiber a day.

Finding Insoluble Fiber

Bran cereals
Brown rice
Corn
Popcorn
Whole-grain breads and pastas

Seeking Soluble Fiber

Apples
Apricots
Barley
Carrots
Dried beans and peas
Figs
Oatmeal and oat bran
Okra
Oranges
Peaches
Psyllium
Strawberries

Fluids

Getting enough fluids every day is crucial to good health, but it's something many people overlook. On an average day, you need at least six to eight 8-ounce glasses of fluid, most of it water. In hot weather and humid climates, and at high altitudes, you'll need even more. Juice and seltzer are also good for fluid replacement, though you'll need to take the calorie counts of juices into account. Tea and coffee count as fluids, but caffeinated versions can also act as diuretics. If you drink too many caffeinated beverages, you could end up with a net loss of fluid. Steer clear of sugary drinks. While they are mostly water, they provide unneeded calories and few, if any, nutrients in return. Don't forget that all foods, but especially fruits and vegetables, are sources of water as well.

How do you know if you're getting enough fluid? Don't depend on your thirst to answer that question. Your fluid reservoir can get low long before your thirst kicks in. The older you get, the more that's true. The only way to know if you're getting enough fluid is to check out the color of your urine. Urinating a light yellow urine every two to four hours tells you you're in good shape. However, if there is little urine and it's dark, you need to be drinking more.

Vitamins

Vitamin A

There are only a handful of foods that provide already-formed vitamin A. These include fortified milk, liver, fish liver oils, and eggs. Preformed vitamin A is also typically found in vitamin supplements. Most vitamin A, however, comes from colorful plant foods, rich in carotenoids, which the body is able to convert to vitamin A. Look for bright orange, red, yellow, and green fruits and vegetables. Their bright colors signal that they are good sources of carotenoids. Many vitamin supplements provide at least a part of the vitamin A they contain in the form of beta-carotene, the carotenoid that is most efficiently converted to vitamin A.

Cranking Up the Carotenoids

Brussels sprouts
Cantaloupe
Carrots
Kale
Mango
Peppers, red or green
Pumpkin
Romaine lettuce
Spinach
Sweet potatoes
Winter squash

Riboflavin

The principle sources of riboflavin in the diet are milk and yogurt, though whole grains, wheat germ, and eggs are rich sources as well. Because riboflavin is sensitive to light, milk stored in see-through plastic jugs and glass containers is likely to have lost some of the vitamin during storage. More riboflavin is likely to be retained in milk sold in cardboard cartons. Most multivitamins provide about 100 percent of the recommended intake for riboflavin, but some "B for-

mula" supplements have even higher levels of all the "B's."

Racking Up Riboflavin

Almonds
Asparagus
Chicken thighs
Fortified breakfast cereals
Milk
Turkey
Wheat germ
Whole-grain or enriched bread
Yogurt

Vitamin B6

Foods rich in protein, such as chicken, fish, and pork, are also rich in vitamin B6. Refined grains are low in vitamin B6 because the B vitamins are generally removed during the refining process. While enriched breads have other B vitamins added back, B6 isn't one of them. Fortified cereals, however, are good sources of the vitamin. Though B6 is considered a safe vitamin, experts discovered several years ago that if you take more than one gram a day for an extended period of time, it can cause a temporary tingling and loss of feeling in your hands and feet. When you stop taking such large amounts, the symptoms should go away.

A Bevy of B6
Bananas
Beef
Bran flakes
Fish
Spinach
Wheat germ

Vitamin B12

Vitamin B12 is unique to animal tissues, so it's not found in plants at all. However, it is added to most fortified breakfast cereals, making them a good source of the vitamin. It takes only a small, 3-ounce serving of lean beef to provide all the vitamin B12 you need for the day. Vegans, vegetarians who shun all animal products, are at risk for a B12 deficiency if they don't also take a vitamin supplement or eat a fortified cereal. Most supplements provide 100 percent of the recommended intake for the

vitamin, but taking larger amounts is safe.

Boosting B12
Beef
Cheese
Chicken
Eggs
Milk
Salmon
Tuna
Turkey

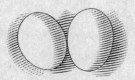

Folate

Folate is one of the rare instances in which the synthetic form is actually better absorbed by the body than the natural form found in foods. So, fortified cereals and vitamin supplements (both of which use folic acid) are excellent sources of folate. In fact, the law requires folic acid to be added to enriched breads and grains. In supplements it is often found in combination with other B vitamins, especially B6 and B12, since they all work together to prevent the buildup of homocysteine in the blood.

Folic Acid Fixes
Asparagus
Bananas
Beets
Chickpeas
Lentils
Orange juice
Spinach
Turnip greens
Wheat germ

Cantaloupe
Cauliflower
Cranberry juice cocktail
Grapefruit
Mango
Orange juice
Peppers, green or red, sweet
Strawberries
Swiss chard
Tomatoes

Vitamin C

Some nutrients are hard to get by diet alone, but vitamin C isn't one of them. Load up on fruits and vegetables, and you've got it made. Even the saturation level of 200 milligrams a day can easily be figured into your daily diet. If you opt for supplements, there is no need to go over 400 milligrams a day, since the extra C appears to offer no health benefit. If you take more than 1,000 milligrams a day, you could trigger diarrhea and cramps.

Stocking Up on C
Broccoli
Brussels sprouts

Vitamin D

Few foods actually contain vitamin D in its ready-to-use form. That's why it's a good idea to get at least some exposure to the sun, which allows your skin to make up the difference by manufacturing D on its own. Besides, it's been found that vitamin D levels in milk are notoriously inconsistent. Some are too high and some are far too low. The bottom line: You can't always depend on milk for the D you need. Supplements generally provide about 100 percent of the recommended intake, but don't double up on food sources and supplements. Limit your intake to an absolute maximum of 2,000 IU a day. Taking more could spell trouble and put you at risk for weakened bones.

Digging Up D in Your Diet
Cod liver oil
Eggs
Fortified breakfast
    cereals
Margarine
Milk

Vitamin E

There's much disagreement over how much E is enough to keep you healthy. The official recommended intake is 10 IU a day, which is easy to obtain from your diet with a little planning. But some experts believe that you need at least ten times that amount for antioxidant protection. Since vitamin E is naturally packaged in fatty foods, you'd need to take vitamin E supplements for higher intakes of the vitamin. Eating too many fatty foods would put you at risk of exceeding your calorie quota. Vitamin E supplements range from doses of 50 IU to 1,000 IU. Supplements of up to 1,000 IU are considered safe. Supplements containing natural, rather than synthetic, vitamin E pack more antioxidant punch per milligram, so opt for natural when you can.

Getting Extra E
Avocados
Kale
Mayonnaise
Olive oil
Spinach
Sunflower seeds
Wheat germ

Minerals

Calcium

Low fat dairy foods are your best bet for getting calcium into your diet. No other natural calcium source can beat an 8-ounce glass of milk or an 8-ounce carton of yogurt (300 milligrams). Some soy milks are fortified with calcium, but they are not naturally rich in calcium. Be sure to read labels carefully. Calcium-fortified orange juice is another calcium-rich option. An 8-ounce glass of fortified orange juice provides as much calcium as an 8-ounce glass of milk. For an extra calcium boost, you can also try adding nonfat dry milk to dishes such as casseroles, cream soups, puddings, breads, pancakes and waffles, and even to already calcium-rich dairy foods such as yogurt, milkshakes, and even a glass of milk. If you're not a fan of dairy, then calcium supplements are your best bet. Try to limit your dosage to no more than 500 milligrams at a time. Research shows that's the dose at which absorption is best. Calcium citrate and calcium citrate malate, the forms found in some supplements and in fortified juices, appear to be among the most absorbable kinds of calcium.

Counting All Calcium
Baked beans
Broccoli
Calcium-fortified orange juice
Calcium-fortified soy milk
Cottage cheese
Ice cream
Kale
Milk
Salmon, canned with bones
Sardines
Tofu
Yogurt

Chromium
You won't find a long list of foods that are rich in chromium. Unrefined foods that aren't overly processed are your best bets, since chromium is often one of the casualties of food processing. Some fortified cereals add chromium to the nutrient mix, making them good sources of the mineral. Multivitamins usually contain 100 percent of the recommended chromium intake. However, there are several supplements that offer chromium in larger amounts for lowering blood sugar and losing weight. Studies show that chromium supplements (chromium picolinate is one of the best-absorbed forms of chromium) may help regulate

blood sugar, but the jury is still out on its effectiveness as a weight-loss aid.

Chromium Cache
American cheese
Beef
Beer
Black pepper
Bran
Brewer's yeast
Broccoli
Chicken
Eggs
Fortified cereals
Oysters
Red wine
Wheat germ

Iron
To keep your iron intake down, limit or avoid iron-fortified foods. Read Nutrition Facts and Supplement Facts labels carefully to avoid forti-fied foods and supplements that contain extra iron. Sup-plements dubbed "senior" or "silver" often have low levels of iron or none at all. Don't take in more meat (a source of the readily absorbed heme

iron) than you need. A small 3-ounce serving a day is plenty.

Identifying Iron
Beef
Dried beans and peas
Fortified cereals
Liver
Molasses, blackstrap
Oysters
Wheat germ

Magnesium
Magnesium is present in a broad selection of plant and animal foods, which should make it fairly easy to get enough in your diet. But mag-nesium intakes are notoriously low because the mineral is usually present in small amounts. Depending on the food choices you make, you could easily be low in the much-needed nutrient. Mag-nesium is also available in some laxatives (think Milk of Magnesia). Most multivitamins contain 100 percent of the recommended intake, but some bone-formula supple-ments provide even more.

Take in too much, however, and you could feel magnesium's laxative effects.

Meet Magnesium

Almonds
Cashews
Lentils
Oatmeal
Peanut butter
Spinach
Sunflower seeds
Wheat germ
Whole-wheat bread

Potassium

Because potassium is present in all plant and animal cells, it's pretty easy to come by in the diet. Among the richest sources, however, are fruits and vegetables. There's no need to take potassium supplements; in fact, they can be deadly, causing the heart to stop beating if you take too much.

Pumping Up Potassium

Apricots, dried
Avocados
Bananas
Chickpeas
Dried beans and peas
Dried plums
Lentils
Milk
Potatoes
Spinach
Tomato juice

Selenium

Probably the best sources of selenium are the strange trio of Brazil nuts, organ meats, and seafood. Selenium also is in a variety of vegetables, but how much depends to a great extent on the level of selenium in the soil in which they were grown. Selenium supplements are okay, but be cautious. More than 1,000 milligrams a day could cause hair loss and nerve damage.

Selecting Selenium

Beef or calf liver
Brazil nuts
Cabbage
Garlic
Halibut
Lobster
Mushrooms

Oysters
Sardines
Shrimp
Wheat germ
Whole-wheat bread

Zinc

Vegetarians may have a bit of trouble getting enough zinc in their diets since red meat is one of the richest sources of the mineral, outdone only by oysters. Fortified cereals almost always have zinc added at levels of about 25 percent of the recommended intake; multivitamins usually have 100 percent or more of the recommended intake. Be sure not to overdo on zinc supplements because you can suppress your immune system as well as lower HDLs (high-density lipoproteins), the "good cholesterol" in your blood.

Zeroing in on Zinc

Beef
Brewer's yeast
Crab
Dried beans
Fortified cereals
Liver
Oysters
Pork
Shrimp
Turkey
Wheat germ

So You Want to Lose Weight

It's time for some straight talk: You weigh more than you did ten years ago, or even five years ago. The extra pounds didn't arrive all at once but accumulated gradually before you even realized they were climbing on board. Now you're looking at some serious extra poundage. But that's to be expected as you get older, right? Wrong.

Putting on excess weight is very common for a number of reasons that we'll explain. But it's not an inevitable part of the aging process, and it could put your health at risk.

If you understand why you tend to gain weight more easily as you get older, you can do something about it. And doing something about it is what this book is all about.

You can blame a lot of your weight gain on your metabolism. Beginning as early as your mid-twenties, body fat begins to increase while muscle mass decreases. And less muscle mass translates into a slower metabolic rate. Muscle mass decreases from about 45 percent of your total body weight in your youth to about 27 percent by the time you reach age 70. And the drop in hormones that accompanies menopause also precipitates a decrease in muscle mass, triggering even more weight gain for women. Your body fat, meanwhile, can double, even if your weight remains the same.

The bottom line is that you burn fewer calories in your 50s, 60s, or 70s doing the same activities, and the same number of them, that you did in your 20s, 30s, or 40s. The key to preventing weight gain is to compensate by adjusting your food intake, exercising, and generally becoming more physically active.

Taking Stock

The best way to determine if you're carrying around too much weight (and probably not enough muscle) is to calculate your body mass index (BMI). BMI is just one indicator of good health, but it's a good place to start. A lower BMI indicates you're more likely to be healthy. Here's how to figure yours:

1. Weigh yourself first thing in the morning, without clothes.
2. Measure your height in inches.
3. Multiply your weight in pounds by 700.
4. Divide the answer in #3 by your height.
5. Divide the answer in #4 by your height again.
6. The answer in #5 is your BMI.

What Your BMI Means:

19–24.9 is a healthy weight
25–29.9 is overweight
30 or more is obese

Knowing how many calories you need each day is another important piece of information that will help you manage your weight. Most experts say that 2,300 calories a day should meet the energy needs of men older than 50 who are moderately active. For women over 50 who are moderately active, 1,900 calories a day should do it. However, these are just ballpark figures. Individual calorie needs can differ greatly depending on muscle mass, physical activity, and genetic differences.

On page 40 you'll find a guide for calculating your calorie needs if you're lightly to moderately active (you're not a couch potato but you don't work out five times a week at the gym, either). You'll need 20 percent to 30 percent more calories if you're very physically active (you regularly participate in competitive sports, run, or go to exercise classes or the gym and spend little time just sitting and watching TV or reading).

While it's true that the more calories you cut, the quicker you'll lose, don't make the mistake of cutting back too much. If you go too low, you won't get enough nutrients, you'll be fatigued, and your body will simply compensate by slowing its metabolic rate even further so that each calorie is used as efficiently as possible. A slower metabolic rate means that your food sacrifices won't amount to the weight loss you expected: You'll have sacrificed for little reward.

For men: Multiply your goal or ideal weight by 13.5 to get your daily calorie needs.

For women: Multiply your goal or ideal weight by 13.2 to get your daily calorie needs.

The Other Half of the Weight-Loss Battle

Managing your weight doesn't just mean counting calories and figuring out your BMI. It also means taking control of your emotions and your food cravings. Most of us discover sooner or later that it's usually emotions and cravings (sometimes triggered by emotions), not an insatiable appetite, that make us overeat. If you uncover the triggers that make

Coping With Cravings

Psychologists have found that most cravings have remarkably similar patterns. They begin slowly, gradually gain intensity, reach a peak, and whether or not you give in, they fade away in a fairly short time. What should you do? Wait out the storm. If you can stop yourself from giving in, the craving will eventually fade away on its own.

you overeat and learn how to manage them, you'll have won half the weight-loss battle. Just be sure the coping techniques you develop are those you can live with. If they aren't, you won't stick with them.

Conquering Cravings

Though there is research suggesting that some cravings may have a biological origin, most are brought on by out-of-control emotions or situations. Here are a few common emotional triggers and tips for gaining control over them.

Anger

If anger (especially suppressed anger) sends you seeking comfort food, then you're managing your anger by overeating. While food may seem like your most dependable source of comfort, it ultimately leaves you more out of sorts than before. Face the source of your anger head on. Once you've done that, it's less likely to blow up and compel you to eat—and overeat.

Stress

Stress, no matter what its source, is a common trigger for overeating. Ask yourself, do you reach for chocolate-chocolate-chip ice cream every time your nosy neighbor calls? Do you pack away the potato chips every time you balance your checkbook? You can't eliminate these triggers from your life, but you can try to reduce the anxiety. First, make sure you get enough sleep. You're more susceptible to stress when you're not rested. Try different relaxation techniques, such as deep breathing, yoga, reading, or listening to soft music—whatever works for you. Try to find other, more positive outlets for your stress.

Boredom

There's nothing on TV tonight, you've already finished reading that novel, and you certainly don't feel like washing dishes or sweeping the kitchen floor. The refrigerator sure looks good right about

Ephedra: Worth the Risk?

There are dozens of supplements that claim to make weight loss quicker and easier. Ephedra, also known as ma huang, is one of them. Though several short-term studies suggest that ephedra does offer a modest boost to weight-loss efforts, long-term studies are necessary to determine if it can work safely over the long haul.

Dozens of reports have shown that it can be risky for some people. And there's no way to know in advance if you are one of them. Anecdotal evidence shows that ephedra can cause a variety of side effects, including nervousness, anxiety, irregular heartbeat, hypertension, insomnia, psychosis, seizures, heart attack, stroke, and even death. Even those who believe it is safe and effective agree that you should not take it if you have coronary thrombosis, diabetes, glaucoma, heart disease,

now! Before you find yourself rummaging through the freezer for ice cream, do whatever it takes to shift the focus away from food. Take a shower, paint your nails, throw out old newspapers, or take one last look through that magazine before you toss it. Make a list of your favorite diversions and keep them posted on the fridge.

Depression

We're talking here about the blue mood that takes hold of everyone now and then. The blues not only prevent us from doing the things we want to do; sometimes they make us do things we'd rather not—such as overeat. Instead of letting that funk make you overeat, view it as a call to action. Getting active is one of

high blood pressure, thyroid disease, impaired circulation in the brain, enlarged prostate, or kidney problems, or if you're also taking over-the-counter decongestants or monoamine oxidase inhibitor drugs including the antidepressants isocarboxazid (Marplan), phenelzine (Nardil), and tranylcypromine (Parnate).

The Food and Drug Administration currently recommends that you avoid taking supplements containing ephedra. But if you do take them, limit your intake to no more than 8 milligrams (mg) of total ephedra alkaloids per dose and your daily intake to 24 mg total to minimize the risk of dangerous side effects. Be aware, though, that you may not know how much ephedra your dose actually contains. At least one study shows that the amount of ephedra in supplements can differ greatly from what the label says.

the best ways for lifting a black cloud. Physical activity may raise levels of endorphins, which are compounds in the brain that promote a sense of well-being, according to John Foreyt, Ph.D., a psychologist and director of the Nutrition Research Clinic at Baylor College of Medicine in Houston. Any exercise will do, just make it regular.

Happiness

Yes, it's true. Even happiness can make you fat. Who doesn't feel like celebrating when something good happens? And celebrations often involve food. That doesn't mean you should never celebrate because you might overeat. Just learn to compensate. If you overeat at a celebratory dinner, simply cut back the next day.

Demystifying Food

Before you can take control of your eating habits, you have to take away the power that food has over you. In the process, you can begin to look at what you put on your plate as a positive power instead of an evil force over which you've lost all control. The following are tips on "de-powerizing" the role food plays in your life from Marsha Hudnall, M.S., R.D., a nutritionist at Green Mountain at Fox Run, the nation's oldest and most respected weight-management retreat for women.

• Think moderation, not elimination. Figure out what's important and what's not. Learn to eat less of the things you enjoy the most. Knowing you can still look forward to your favorite foods makes the process something you can live with for a lifetime.

• Eat regularly in response to real hunger. Learn to listen to your body's cues. By eating healthful, balanced meals and snacks when you're hungry, you're less likely to get caught up in out-of-control eating that you'll regret later.

• Say good-bye to calorie counting. Switch your focus from calories to good nutrition. Make your healthful eating changes gradual, so you don't get overwhelmed.

• Picture portions. It's hard to manage your food intake if you don't have a clue what a ½ cup serving of pasta looks like or what a 6-ounce glass of juice is. When you start out, measure your food until you've learned to judge portion sizes accurately. If portion sizes start creeping back up, return to measuring and weighing for a while.

• Disconnect with the scale. Don't focus on a number, instead use how you feel and the way your clothes fit to measure success. If you just can't give up the scale, make your weigh-ins less frequent.

Moving Toward Weight Control

If you're determined to succeed at losing weight, simply cutting calories won't guarantee success. Physical activity is as essential to achieving long-term weight loss as a healthful diet, according to the National Institutes of Health (NIH). By themselves, neither exercise nor diet can get you to your goal as effectively or as fast as the two of them can together. That's especially true for people over age 50.

Not only is physical activity essential for weight-loss success, the NIH says it's an important factor in maintaining your weight once you've lost the extra pounds. Take comfort in the NIH's use of the words "physical activity," not "exercise." The message is that you can win the weight-loss game with many different kinds of physical activity. You don't have to do killer aerobics and lift heavy weights at a gym to drop pounds and keep them off. But you do have to do something, and you have to do it regularly.

Anti-Aging Bonus

Researchers have recently learned that regular physical activity can have a powerful effect on age-related declines in metabolism. One study out of Tufts University Center for Physical Fitness found that strength training by itself increased the metabolic rate of postmenopausal women by 15 percent. Not much, you say? If the boost translates to only 100 calories a day, which is a realistic expectation, you could save yourself from putting on an extra 10 pounds in a year.

Regular exercise offers a trifecta of good health: It burns calories, builds muscle, and improves your overall health. Experts on aging say that the body is better able to repair itself and perform efficiently if it is properly conditioned by exercise and good nutrition. And the calorie-burning rewards of exercise are not limited to your workout time. Some research suggests that your revved up metabolic rate stays elevated for several hours after you stop exercising.

While weight management may be your number one priority now, think fitness not thinness. Just look at all the other health bonuses experts attribute to being physically active:

Regular physical activity reduces your risk of developing

- heart disease
- some kinds of cancer
- high blood pressure
- osteoporosis
- diabetes
- obesity

It also can reduce the symptoms of

- arthritis
- anxiety
- depression
- insomnia

And it boosts and builds

- the immune system
- your energy level
- your muscle mass
- blood flow to the brain, which helps keep you mentally sharp

Choose to Move

So how should you get started? It doesn't matter how you begin, just get moving! Any activity is better than vegetating in front of the television. Look for every opportunity you can to stand instead of sit, walk instead of drive, or run instead of walk. Turn your everyday activities into opportunities for physical activity, and make movement a routine part of your everyday life.

Triad of Physical Activity

Recent research has found that when it comes to exercise, you need a combination of three types to reap the most health benefits—weight training for strength, aerobic exercise for strength and endurance, and calisthenics (stretching, bending, and twisting exercises) for flexibility. Studies have found that extreme physical exertion is no more useful to gaining and maintaining fitness than is moderate exercise. What's more, you place yourself at risk for injury or a heart attack if you're not already in good physical shape. So start off slowly and increase your activity gradually.

Step Up to Good Health

One of the easiest ways to get physically active is to walk at a pace that makes you breathe a little harder and work up a mild sweat for 30 minutes to 1 hour three days a week. This kind of walking will keep your heart, lungs, and vascular system in good working order and strengthen your bones and muscles. If you just don't have time for a 30-minute walk each day, experts say that walking about 10,000 steps a day (the equivalent of about five miles) while doing your normal activities should keep you fit. Haven't a clue how much walking that is? Try using a pedometer. It's a small battery-operated gizmo about the size of a matchbox that you attach to your waist so it can monitor your every step. By keeping track of your movements all day, you can easily see how far you've gone and how far you have yet to go to reach your goal.

Swim Your Way to Fitness

If you have arthritis that makes some movements painful, swimming is an excellent way to get aerobically fit. It offers some of the same benefits as walking or other aerobic exercises without putting stress on joints that may be unable to repair themselves like healthy joints would. The one benefit swimming can't provide, how-

Calories Burned

If you're exercising to lose weight, it's helpful to know how many calories you're burning. Use this chart to gauge the weight-loss effects of your efforts.

Activity (1 hour)	135 lbs	155 lbs	190 lbs
Aerobics	354	422	518
Bicycling, leisurely	236	281	345
Bicycling, stationary	295	352	431
Bowling	177	211	259
Cleaning house	207	246	302
Running (6 mph; 10-min. mile)	590	704	863
Skating, ice	413	493	604
Stair-treadmill	354	422	518
Swimming	236	281	345
Walking, 3 mph	207	246	302
Weight lifting	177	211	259

ever, is strengthening bones because it is not a weight-bearing exercise.

Not Just for Bodybuilders
If you think lifting weights is just for 20-something Schwarzenegger wannabes, think again. It's a little-appreciated fact that muscle tissue burns more calories than fat tissue does, even when at rest. The more muscle you have, the more calories you burn.

Since muscle mass declines with age—typically about five percent per decade beginning in your late twenties or early thirties—it's to your advantage to try to increase your muscle mass through strength training. The older you get, the greater the potential benefit. So, as the saying goes, use it or lose it.

Research from the United States Department of Agriculture (USDA) recently confirmed that the gradual loss of muscle mass that occurs with age means a decreasing need for calories—and sometimes a creeping weight gain if you don't lower your calorie intake. The more you can do to minimize the effect of muscle loss, whether it's due to age, inactivity, or both, the easier weight loss will be. But before you start trying to bench-press your own body weight, it's important to distinguish between true weight lifting and strength training. Weight lifting is about bulking up so you can lift heavy weights swiftly. Strength training, on the other hand, is about firming by repeatedly lifting weights in a very slow, controlled way. It's a good idea when you first get started to have a trainer show you exactly how it should be done to avoid injury. Your training can be done with free weights, such as barbells, or with specially designed equipment that works specific parts of the body. You should do a set number of repetitions with each exercise as you slowly progress to your goal. Muscle strengthening exercises should be done for at least 20 minutes, three times a week.

Where to Get Started

Don't want to fork over the cash for a high-class health club? Many kinds of organizations, such as the YMCA and

YWCA, junior colleges and universities, senior and community centers, and adult and continuing education programs, offer inexpensive classes in sports, exercise, dance, and weight training. The instructors in these classes can help you get the most benefit from exercise while avoiding injury. Attend with a friend; you're more likely to stick with it if you know you have a partner waiting for you.

Your Power Source

When you're increasing your physical activity, don't drastically cut your calorie intake. Of course, you have to cut calories to lose weight—just don't get carried away. Fewer than 1,500 calories a day may not leave you with enough energy to make it through a regular day, much less a day filled with more physical activity than you're used to. And make sure 40 to 60 percent of those calories come from carbohydrates, the chief power source for your body and your brain. Diets that ban carbohydrates could leave you with a power-draining energy deficit.

Do You Need More Protein?

It's a myth that you need more protein if you're going to be more active and build muscle. Only serious athletes require more protein than the rest of us, and even then it's not a lot more. Most of us can get all the protein we need in a day from about three ounces of lean meat, even less if the diet includes other high-protein foods such as eggs, low fat milk, soybeans, fish, and dried beans. So, don't waste your money on high-protein shakes that promise to bulk you up. Best advice? Be physically active and start a strength-training routine.

Choosing the Best Diet for You

You may be committed to losing weight, but are you stymied by the number of diet plans out there? This time you want to be successful, and you don't want to waste your time on some gimmicky diet that can't deliver on its promises. And you don't want to embark on a plan that doesn't fit your personality, either. Picking a healthful diet that can help you drop pounds AND choosing a diet you can live with long term are equally important.

The most important factor to consider is whether the diet is healthy. If it isn't, it doesn't matter whether it's easy to follow, lets you eat your favorite foods, or is inexpensive. Once you've eliminated the diets that are detrimental to your health, you'll find that most have their good points and their bad points. Personal preference, lifestyle, cost, and simplicity will all influence your decision. That's why the diet you choose for yourself may not be the same one your best friend or your coworker chooses.

This chapter will give you the tools you need to weigh the pros and cons of diet plans you're considering. First we offer a series of questions whose answers will help you size up any diet's safety, efficacy, and practicality. And then we'll ask you to think about yourself, quizzing you about your likes and dislikes, your habits, and your lifestyle, so you can eliminate diets you just won't get along with. The end of the chapter addresses special diet considerations you should be aware of if you have any medical problems, such as cardiovascular disease, high blood pressure, or osteoporosis.

The answers to the following questions will raise the red flags and highlight the positive features of any diet plan you're contemplating:

Is it safe?

Watch out if the diet encourages you to take a lot of supplements that haven't been proven to assist weight loss or requires strange food combinations or extremely high levels of protein. Believe it or not, most dietary supplements sold today have not been proven safe or effective. Most food-combining diets are so difficult to follow that you're liable to end up eating a diet that's unhealthy and possibly unsafe. High-protein diets promote ketosis, a metabolic state similar to starvation, which can be hard on your kidneys, toxic to the liver, and deficient in carbohydrates that provide essential instant energy for the brain.

Is it nutritionally sound?

A diet should include all the recommended intakes for vitamins, minerals, and protein (shown as Daily Value, or DV, on food labels). Diets that severely limit food choices or eliminate whole food groups, such as dairy, are unlikely to meet your nutritional needs. For example, diets that are extremely low in fat can be low in fat-soluble vitamins and essential fatty acids, and diets that ban dairy products may be low in vitamin D and calcium. Make sure that the diet takes into consideration the unique nutritional needs of people over age 50.

Does it make sense?

If a diet sounds like the answer to your prayers, watch out. If it says it's going to do what no diet has ever done before, you can be sure it won't. If it claims there is a medical conspiracy preventing you from hearing the truth about weight loss, you can be sure you won't find the truth you're seeking with this diet. There is no "hidden medical secret" and no such thing as instant weight loss. Let your common sense be your guide.

Does it require specially purchased foods?

For a diet to have any hope for long-term success, it's got to incorporate foods you can buy from the supermarket where you usually shop. Short-term use of prepackaged meals is OK and can actually help kick-start some people's efforts. However, if the plan requires you to buy special foods or supplements forever, forget it.

Who's behind the diet?

Was the diet written or developed by a credentialed doctor or nutritionist? While those credentials don't guarantee that the diet provides good dietary guidance (some of the most popular but unsound diets have come from medical doctors), they do slightly increase the odds that the diet will be a sound one that you can stick with over the long haul. But if the diet promotes a certain brand of supplements or a particular brand of meal replacement, for example, you can be fairly certain that the advice is heavily influenced by a sponsor and not by the expert—and it's likely to be expensive to follow.

Does it promise rapid weight loss?

Rapid weight loss often means rapid regain, especially because much of the initial weight loss on crash diets is water loss, not fat. When you start to eat more normally, the pounds will creep back. Most experts recommend a slow and steady weight loss of about a pound or two each week. On any diet you'll probably lose more rapidly at first. After the first couple of weeks the pounds are likely to come off more slowly.

But if rapid weight loss continues, you're inviting long-term failure. Only slow and sure can win the race.

Is it practical?

Does the meal plan offer concrete suggestions for what you can eat as well as substitutes you can make when you're away from home? Does it allow for special occasions, eating out, and feeding other family members? Any diet that doesn't take changing circumstances into consideration isn't worth the time or the effort. The more tips and how-to information the diet book or program provides, the better your chances of sticking with it over the long haul.

Does it require a lot of calculations?

Eating isn't a one-time event; it's a recurring activity throughout each day. Many people don't have time to weigh every morsel, keep a running log of calorie intake, or play a Rubik's Cube game of food balancing.

A good diet plan should lead you through an initial phase of educating yourself about healthy foods and serving sizes. After that, little if any number crunching should be necessary.

Does the diet make physical activity an inseparable part of the plan?

If not, say *hasta la vista*, baby, because you'll go nowhere. Cutting calories and losing weight without physical activity is a temporary solution, at best. Any diet plan that ignores or gives short shrift to this critical aspect of weight management is missing the boat and will set you up for weight-loss failure.

Is a maintenance program included in the diet plan?

No? Then it's like being abandoned without a map by a tour guide when you're halfway to your destination. Losing the weight is a short phase of the diet plan. Maintaining that weight loss is something you'll be doing forever.

Does the diet allow you to individualize the plan?

If you're a 150-pound woman trying to lose 10 pounds, you shouldn't be eating the same diet as a 250-pound man trying to lose 50 pounds. Make sure the diet plan lets you figure the amount of food you can eat and allows for substitutions. If the diet plan makes tofu and grapefruit de rigueur for breakfast and you can abide neither, then you have a problem.

Does the diet plan suggest you check with your doctor first?

If you plan to lose more than 15 to 20 pounds, if you have any existing health problems, or if you take medication on a regular basis, you should check with your doctor first before starting any weight-loss program.

What's the Best Diet for You?

Picking a healthy, practical diet can be a tough job, especially considering all the choices out there. But there's more to selecting a diet plan than that. Diets have their unique personalities and characteristics, and so do you. The trick is finding one that, like your best friend or mate, feels comfortable. You've already read about how to evaluate diets for safety, effectiveness, and nutritional content. Now you need to get personal. Even if the diet is safe, effective, and nutritious, is it really right for you? Only you can accurately answer that question. Your answers to the questions below will lead you to a diet you can stick with.

Take the following self-quiz to determine the type of diet that's right for you.

Diet Determination Quiz

Do you live by the clock? Can't function without your *Day Runner*?

If you answered yes, then you're better off with a diet that offers structure and a lot of direction, including preplanned menus and specific suggestions for substitutions. Some diets leave a lot of the decision-making up to the dieter, but if structure and planning are your life, those won't be right for you. Opt for a diet that sets it all out for you and leaves little to chance.

Are you a spur-of-the-moment kind of person? Hate to plan ahead?

If this describes you, then look for a diet plan that gives you some room to maneuver. If meals have to be planned in advance according to strict guidelines, then your go-with-the-flow lifestyle may doom you to failure before you even begin. Just because you want to lose weight doesn't mean you're going to alter your personality in the process.

Is the main ingredient in the diet one that you hate?

If the diet calls for cabbage at every meal and the smell of cooking cabbage makes you nauseated, then you're barking up the wrong diet tree. Be realistic. Just because it worked for your nearest and dearest friend (who loves cabbage) doesn't mean it's the right diet for you.

Do you prefer a lot of food flexibility or would you rather have your meals pre-determined?

If you want to be led, step by step, through a diet plan, complete with sample menus, recipes, and lists of substitutions, you better make sure that the diet you're considering does just that. Some provide great visuals, grocery lists, and recipes. Others give broad, sweeping guidelines and leave the details up to you.

Do you even know how to operate the oven?

If you eat out most nights of the week and the diet calls for preparation of elaborate recipes for dinner each night, forget it. You'll be much better off if you find a diet that explains how to eat out while still sticking with the diet.

How's your budget?

If your budget is limited and the menus call for special ingredients from gourmet shops or organic ingredients from pricey health-food super-markets, you won't be able to stick with it for long, at least not without cutting back on other expenses. The same holds true for diet programs that charge initiation fees and require you to buy prepack-aged foods.

Do you have any existing health problems?

If you have any medical condi-tions, such as diabetes, heart disease, kidney disease, a neu-rological disorder, or high blood pressure, be sure to check with your health care provider first to make sure the diet you're considering is safe for you. Even if you've gotten your doctor's OK, make sure the diet meets your special nutritional needs, not only because you're past 50 but to accommodate your medical condition. Check out the

"Special Dieting Considera-tions," page 59, for the nutri-ents you need to watch out for.

Be honest. Is this a diet you believe you can stick with forever?

While success is often mistak-enly measured by weight loss, the real key to success is weight maintenance—keeping the weight off once you've lost it. If the diet is too strict or too monotonous, leaves you drained of energy, or is just too weird for you, you won't stay with it. Give this some serious thought before you get started, so you don't face the all-too-familiar (and unhealthy) ups and downs of yo-yo dieting.

Do you need a strong sup-port system?

If yes, then be sure the diet program offers counseling or the diet plan provides enough motivational and helpful resources to get you through. Or, be sure you put your own support system in place before you start. Your support person can be a close friend, a family member, or an online counselor at one of the dieting Web sites (see Resources, page 189).

Is the physical activity portion of the program something you can keep up with?
If the diet has led you to believe you're going to have "buns of steel" or "six-pack abs" from your weight-loss and exercise programs, toss the diet in the trash. Your goal should be a healthier, fitter you, not some supreme level of physical fitness.

Do you hate to count calories?
Then don't even try to stick with a diet that has you thumbing through calorie-counting books all day and keeping a running tally on every calorie you put in your mouth. Instead, look for a diet that focuses on balancing foods and food groups, not counting calories. It never hurts to get familiar with the calorie counts of foods so there are no high-calorie surprises, but there's no need to live by calorie-counting rules if it's just not you. You'll be much better off in the long run.

Do you live alone or with a partner, roommate, kids, or grandkids?
Your family situation can either limit or broaden your dieting possibilities. Kids probably present the biggest obstacle to healthy eating. And their activity level and rapid metabolism allow them to get away with eating junk food along with all the healthy stuff. You should be so lucky. A diet that forbids treats of any kind may not be realistic when you keep them in the house for the kids. But kids aren't the only problem. Spouses can be, too. A 225-pound man who stays fit will, due to sheer size and muscle mass, be able to eat almost twice a woman's food allowance. Make sure the diet educates you on portion sizes so you won't be influenced by his double portion sizes.

Whatever your living arrangements, make sure you take them into consideration when you choose an eating plan. It may affect everyone else in the household.

When you check out the diet plan, does something just not seem quite right?
Go with your instincts. If you don't feel comfortable and confident about your diet plan in the beginning, you probably never will. It should be "love at first sight." The initial excitement may eventually wear off, but somehow you'll know it's something you can live with forever.

Special Dieting Considerations

If you suffer from any medical condition, you should check with your doctor before beginning any new diet plan. If you're given the green light, here are a few finer points to watch out for when trying to choose the diet that's best for you.

Cardiovascular Disease

If high cholesterol or a history of heart disease is an issue, steer clear of diets that encourage you to eat a lot of animal products. Only animal products contain cholesterol, and they are the primary sources of saturated fats—two dietary components that you need to keep to a minimum. Make sure the diet includes lots of fruits and vegetables, as they contain an arsenal of phytochemicals that may help keep your heart healthy. And make sure you're getting plenty of folic acid and vitamins B_6 and B_{12} from food or supplements, since this trio of "B's" has been shown to control homocysteine levels in the blood. High homocysteine levels increase your risk of clogged arteries and heart disease.

Breast Cancer

Though it's far from proven, some experts believe that women at risk for breast cancer should not consume a lot of soy products. That's because soy is one of the richest sources of isoflavones, naturally occurring compounds that have an estrogenlike action in the body. Some tumors are estrogen-dependent and feed off the hormone to survive. Too much estrogen could increase the risk. Though the "proof" so far comes only from animal and lab studies, some experts say, why risk it?

Constipation

If constipation is an issue for you, steer clear of diets that discourage the consumption of carbohydrates, such as high-fiber whole grains, or that limit your intake of fruits and vegetables. Try to get 20 to 35 grams of fiber a day from whichever diet plan you choose.

Diabetes

Don't tempt fate by trying any sort of unbalanced diet plan that emphasizes any one food or food group over another. Choose a diet plan that includes enough—but not too much—protein, carbohydrates, and fat. Because diabetes puts you at increased risk for heart disease, opt for a diet that emphasizes heart-healthy monounsaturated and polyunsaturated fats and that includes a healthy dose of soluble fiber from beans, peas, lentils, oats, fruits, and vegetables. These foods will help keep both blood sugar and blood cholesterol under control.

Gallstones

Make sure you plan on sticking with your diet and maintaining your weight loss. Research shows that "weight cyclers," also known as yo-yo dieters, are putting themselves at risk for developing gallstones. If you already suffer from gallstones, you could make matters worse.

High Blood Pressure

If your blood pressure tends to be high, you're at an increased risk for a heart attack or stroke. The diet that offers the best protection against high blood pressure includes plenty of low fat dairy foods and lots of fruits and vegetables. The key nutrients to focus on? Calcium, potassium, and magnesium. And go easy on the salt. Aim each day to eat at least 4 to 5 servings of vegetables; 4 to 5 servings of fruits; 7 to 8 servings of grains; 2 to 3 servings of nonfat dairy; no more than 2 servings a day of fish, poultry, or lean meat; 4 to 5 servings a week of nuts, seeds, and beans.

Kidney Disease

There are many different kinds of kidney disease, so it's best to check with your doctor before you try any new diet plan. But in general, if you have kidney troubles, don't consume too much protein. That means you should steer clear of diet plans that emphasize eating meat, fish, and poultry. People with kidney disease should drink plenty of fluids to decrease the risk of developing kidney stones and bladder cancer.

Osteoporosis

Calcium and vitamin D are vital to the prevention of this debilitating, bone-robbing disease, so make sure that whatever diet you choose includes plenty of those two bone-building nutrients. And make sure the diet's not heavy on protein or sodium consumption, since both can leech the calcium right out of your bones, leaving them weak, brittle, and prone to fractures.

The Age-Free Zone

The Premise

With a few modifications of his original *The Zone* diet book, Dr. Barry Sears has come up with an anti-aging diet plan that can help you lose weight. Sears believes that excess amounts of insulin, blood glucose, cortisol, and free radicals are responsible for the aging process, and his plan is designed to reduce and control them via diet and lifestyle. Though the diet isn't a weight-loss plan per se, calorie restriction is a critical part of it. That's because Sears believes calorie restriction is a guaranteed anti-aging tool. The *Age-Free Zone* has a diet and lifestyle pyramid, which includes meditation, moderate exercise, and of course, the Zone diet. But the real focus here is on cutting calories by reducing total carbohydrate intake and eliminating simple carbohydrates. The point is to control insulin, although the plan covers control of several other hormones, including thyroid, estrogen, progesterone, growth hormone, testosterone, DHEA, and melatonin, all of which lead to accelerated aging and weight gain, according to Sears.

Quick Take

- Low-carbohydrate, high-protein, calorie-restricted diet

- Designed to control hormones, especially insulin, to delay aging

- Includes a detailed pre-scription for dietary supplements

This Diet Is Best for: People who can't give up or cut back on animal foods, such as meat and chicken, and those who want to cut back on but not severely restrict their carbohydrate intake

Who Should Not Try This Diet: Anyone who needs to watch their protein intake, such as people with kidney problems, should not follow the diet without their doctor's advice. Although the diet is recommended for people with Type 2 diabetes, it is much lower in carbohydrates than what most experts recommend. If you have diabetes, check with your doctor before starting the diet.

The Rationale

Sears' anti-aging theory claims that calorie restriction not only helps you lose weight but also reduces free radical production and excess blood glucose and insulin levels. All of these can be detrimental to your health. The key to effective calorie restriction, says Sears, is to determine the minimum level of carbohydrate you need to function efficiently. Sticking to the minimum will allow the body to perform its daily functions without causing overproduction of free radicals, glucose, or insulin. In addition to a low-carbohydrate, high-protein diet, Sears recommends a wide variety of antioxidant, anti-aging supplements. However, food and exercise are Sears' ultimate "drugs" of choice to control and reduce excess hormone production.

What's for Breakfast, Lunch, and Dinner?

The diet plan is divided into three meals and two snacks a day. Meals consist of three choices from each group (protein, carbohydrate, and fat) for women and four choices from each group for men. The diet book provides two weeks' worth of menus, as well as several recipes that are incorporated into the sample menus. A typical day's menus might include soy patties, low-fat cheese, and fruit salad for breakfast; tossed salad with oil and vinegar dressing, turkey breast, reduced-fat cheese, and a pear for lunch; fish, olive oil, tomatoes with Parmesan cheese, green beans, and grapes for dinner; and two snacks during the day. The book also provides brief lists of protein, carbohydrate, fat, and snack choices around which you can plan your meals. The basic Zone meal guidelines are: 1. Always eat within one hour after waking. 2. Never let more than five hours go by without eating a Zone meal or snack, whether you are hungry or not. 3. Include some protein at every meal and snack. 4. Eat more fruits and vegetables, and ease off the bread, pasta, grains, and starches. 5. Always eat your snack. 6. Drink at least 64 ounces of liquid each day. 7. Eat a snack 30 minutes before exercise.

> ### Calorie Quota
> Women should consume about 1,200 calories a day; men about 1,500 calories day.

Fact or Fiction: What the Experts Say

Despite Sears' claim that determining the minimum amount of carbohydrate is key to forestalling aging, he gives no general recommendations for how to determine that intake nor any specifics about how to tailor the diet plan to meet your own needs. Though much of what Sears says about free radical damage, insulin levels, and calorie restriction is based on research studies, he carries the theory a couple of steps beyond what research has actually shown. He recommends a lot of unnecessary and potentially dangerous combinations of supplements to augment his anti-aging program.

NO-NO'S

High-carbohydrate foods, high fat foods, processed foods, low-fiber foods

Gains and Losses/ What's the Damage?

If you follow Sears' diet plan of 1,200 calories a day for women and 1,500 calories a day for men, you should be able to lose weight, but you could fall short on some important nutrients, such as B vitamins and calcium, which are particularly important for the over-50 dieter. However, Sears does recommend vitamin and mineral supplements, including calcium, to make up the difference. Still, the diet is too high in protein and too low in complex carbohydrates and fiber, which could leave you low on energy and constipated. And while Sears advocates the diet for people with Type 2 diabetes, most

YES-YES'S

Calorie restriction; fruits, vegetables, protein at each meal and snack; a limited amount of complex carbohydrates; healthy fats

diabetes experts recommend a diet much higher in carbohydrates than the plan provided in the book.

Other Similar Diets

SugarBusters!; Eat More, Weigh Less; Dr. Atkins' Age Defying Diet Revolution; Eat, Drink, and Be Healthy

Dr. Atkins' Age-Defying Diet Revolution

The Premise

Atkins, of high-protein diet fame, has made a foray into anti-aging nutrition with this diet plan. He rightly contends that chronic disease, such as heart disease, diabetes, and high blood pressure, accelerates the aging process no matter what your age. But defying the "prevailing beliefs" about aging, Atkins maintains that most of the physical and mental decline that we consider an inevitable part of aging is actually avoidable. He blames the current medical establishment for presenting the public with "horribly misleading" information about disease prevention and health. He promises to be the first physician/author to tell readers the "hard truth" that excessive intake of refined carbohydrates

This Diet Is Best for: No one. It's full of half-truths, inadequate instructions about how to follow the diet, and a variety of supplement plans that encourage overconsumption of some compounds.

Who Should Not Try This Diet: Everyone should avoid this diet. It's the same high-protein, low-carbohydrate diet, with an anti-aging twist, that nutritionists have been warning against for 30 years now.

shortens your life. The basis of Atkins' plan, like that of his other books, is a low-carbohydrate, high-protein diet, but this one has an antioxidant twist. He maintains that antioxidants such as vitamins C and E, lipoic acid, and selenium are critical to holding back the hands of time, and he lays out a plan for how to build up your antioxidant shield. Atkins focuses on preventing two major killers: heart disease and diabetes. He does this in part by emphasizing the control of fat levels in the blood, especially high-density lipoprotein (HDL) and triglycerides.

Calorie Quota

There is no calorie counting, nor is there portion size guidance or a food exchange plan. In fact, Atkins discourages all three. He suggests you "eat the amount that makes you feel comfortable."

diseases, and keep you younger longer. The diet focuses on protein and avoids carbohydrates, especially those with a high glycemic index (foods that raise blood sugar levels the most). Avoiding high glycemic index foods is important because Atkins blames overconsumption of those foods for heart disease and diabetes. His theory is that eating high glycemic index foods can trigger insulin resistance, hyperinsulinemia (high levels of insulin in the blood), high blood sugar, and ultimately diabetes. Controlling insulin, says Atkins, is the key to forestalling aging.

The Rationale

Atkins believes that his diet, coupled with an array of supplements, can boost your immunity, fend off chronic

What's for Breakfast, Lunch, and Dinner?

While Atkins talks a lot about foods that are rich in antioxidants, preaches the avoidance of refined carbohydrates, and promotes several different supplement regimens, there is little guidance about exactly what you should put on your plate at each meal. Milk consumption is discouraged because it contains lactose, a simple sugar, but cream is encouraged. Fresh fruit is limited, and fruit juice is eliminated. For weight loss, Atkins suggests a total of 60 grams of carbohydrates a day, but he offers little information on the carbohydrate content of foods.

is no exception. It follows the same pattern as his other diet books, in which he advocates a high protein intake and greatly restricts carbohydrates, especially those from table sugar and refined and processed foods. A diet so low in carbohydrates can leave you feeling drained of energy and is seldom successful over the long-term. In addition, his over-the-top supplementation plans could easily lead to overdosing.

Quick Take

- A high-protein, low-carbohydrate diet

- Eliminates all refined carbohydrates and limits other carbohydrate sources

- Does not require calorie counting; only counts grams of carbohydrates

- Encourages taking a variety of supplements

Fact or Fiction: What the Experts Say

Few health and nutrition experts are fans of any of Atkins' diet plans, and this one

Gains and Losses/ What's the Damage?

Because little guidance is given in terms of what the daily diet should be, it's hard to say if you'll lose weight on the plan. It would be easy to overeat or to fall short on some important

NO-NO'S

High-carbohydrate foods, especially refined carbs and those with a high glycemic index; milk and fresh fruit; fruit juice

YES-YES'S

High-protein foods, cream, low-carbohydrate vegetables, small amounts of whole grains (within the total grams of carbohydrate allowed), a wide variety of supplements

which is for weight loss. But it doesn't say what to do if, for example, you want to lose

nutrients, such as calcium and vitamin D. Almost no mention is made of either of these nutrients in the diet. Calcium-rich milk is limited to one cup a day. Without supplements, that's a sure-fire diet prescription for inadequate calcium and vitamin D intake, which can be bad news for bone health as you age. The diet unwisely encourages the consumption of some foods high in saturated fat, such as cream, which is not a good idea for someone trying to prevent heart disease. Aside from the haphazard and sometimes inaccurate diet advice, the book offers no less than 12 supplement plans for a variety of health conditions, one of

weight while at the same time supplementing for diabetes, a common predicament for people over 50. Because the diet emphasizes protein foods and limits high-fiber whole grains, constipation could be a problem. In addition, a diet so high in animal protein could also be risky for seniors who need to limit, not increase, their iron intake.

Other Similar Diets

The Zone, Dr. Atkins' New Diet Revolution

The Carbohydrate Addict's Lifespan Program

The Premise

This is the latest in a series of seven diet books written by the husband and wife team of Richard and Rachael Heller. Most of these books are follow-ups to their original 1991 book, *The Carbohydrate Addict's Diet*. This updated version, written for the over-40 reader, is basically the same song with some different verses. The Hellers believe that 75 percent of overweight people—and many people of normal weight—are addicted to carbohydrates and that dealing with that addiction is the key to successful weight loss. They define carbohydrate addiction as a compelling hunger, craving, or desire for carbohydrate-rich foods: an escalating, recurring need or drive for starches, snack foods, junk food, or sweets. The Hellers maintain that eating carbohydrates for some people is like doing drugs, and they have devised a diet plan that greatly restricts carbohydrate intake, distributing it in measured amounts at a single meal.

> ### Calorie Quota
> Calories are not counted and there is no limit on calorie intake, but proportions of foods at each meal are controlled.

The Rationale

According to the Hellers, overproduction of insulin is what triggers hunger and drives the carbohydrate addiction. Eating too many carbohydrates, they say, causes a spike in insulin production, triggering carbohydrate cravings. This drives you to eat even more carbohydrates, which creates a never-ending cycle of craving, overconsumption of carbohydrates, and overproduction of insulin. An overindulgence in carbohydrate-rich foods, then, leads to weight gain and out-of-control eating. Their answer is to regulate and restrict carbohydrate intake, especially eliminating foods that contain refined carbs such as sugar and flour.

What's for Breakfast, Lunch, and Dinner?

Though the Hellers' plan is basically a low-carb diet, it doesn't restrict carbohydrates to the degree that the Atkins diet does. In fact, it allows for a single carbohydrate-rich meal each day. Their diet prescription calls for two no-carb meals and one controlled-carbohydrate meal (called a reward meal) each day. The

This Diet Is Best for: Those who have trouble controlling cravings for carbohydrate foods. That's not because the diet magically alters metabolism and reduces cravings but because it restricts carbohydrate intake to only one meal a day. It also is best suited for those who can't deal with the virtual ban on carbohydrates required on the Atkins diet but still want to control their carbohydrate intake.

Who Should Not Try This Diet: Anyone with preexisting health conditions, such as diabetes, heart disease, and kidney disease.

reward meal consists of one-third protein-rich foods, one-third carbohydrate-rich foods, and one-third non-starchy vegetables. You can eat as much as you want, but you must eat it all within a one-hour time limit. The Hellers recommend complex carbohydrates such as pasta, bread, and potatoes. Sugar is not on the menu. Once you've lost the weight, the plan allows you to add carbohydrates to your reward meal a little at a time if you're maintaining your weight.

Fact or Fiction: What the Experts Say

While the "insulin-makes-you-fat" theory is a popular one, researchers have actually found that managing insulin levels does not help you lose weight. But it has been proved that losing weight can help control insulin levels. According to Gerald Reaven, M.D., professor of medicine at Stanford University School of Medicine and an expert on insulin metabolism, "The whole thing is mumbo-jumbo. A calorie is a calorie; if you take in more than you need, you gain weight." Moreover, the Carbohydrate Addict's Quiz that's supposed to diagnose your carbohydrate addiction could diagnose almost everybody because it asks questions like, "Does the sight, smell, or even the thought of food sometimes stimulate you to eat?" Most people could answer yes to this question.

Quick Take

- Maintains that excessive production of insulin triggers carbohydrate cravings, making you overeat

- Restricts carbohydrate intake to control your cravings and help you lose weight

- Requires that you eat foods in particular proportions to one another

Gains and Losses/ What's the Damage?

Though not as extreme as Atkins' diet, the Hellers' diet plan is just as likely to be low in calcium and fiber and high in cholesterol-raising saturated fat, making it bad for your bones and your heart and potentially causing constipation. The symptoms that the Hellers attribute to carbohydrate craving, such as weakness, irritability, and dizziness, could be due to any number of medical conditions and should be checked out by your health care provider. Ironically, the lack of concentration that they attribute to overindulging on carbohydrates is actually a symptom of not getting enough of them. That's because glucose, the sugar the body manufactures from the carbohydrates you eat, is the brain's primary fuel. Like the other low-carb diets, the Hellers' plan is likely to result in weight loss, at least in the beginning. But the high-protein, high fat program is not the best choice for folks over 50 for several reasons.

First, a lot of high-protein meat means a high intake of iron, something you don't need more of at this stage of your life. Too much protein is also bad for your kidneys, as with age they become less efficient at clearing out protein's waste products. Lastly, this diet can mean you get too much of the wrong kind of fat, which is bad for your heart.

NO-NO'S
Sugar-fat combinations and a lot of high-carb foods

YES-YES'S
High-protein, high fat foods

Other Similar Diets

The Atkins' Lifespan Program, The Zone, SugarBusters!

Choose to Lose

The Premise

The Goors have been writing and rewriting their *Choose to Lose* series for the past 15 years. Billed as a "food lover's guide to permanent weight loss," this 500+ page volume tells you everything you need to know, and more, about eating healthy and losing weight. Taking the opposite tact of many diet books, *Choose to Lose* encourages carbohydrate consumption, as long as most of it comes from fruits, vegetables, and whole grains. The focus of the diet is fat: finding it, counting it, and budgeting it. It explains how to plan your own personal fat budget, read food labels, ferret out the fat in the foods you eat, fat-proof your home, eat out healthfully, and switch to healthy fats. They encourage dieters to keep a food diary, at least in the beginning, to learn about their own food habits and to

---

Quick Take

- A balanced diet that includes a wide variety of foods

- Encourages fresh foods but makes great allowances for convenience foods

- Allows occasional splurges

- Encourages exercise

- Not just a weight-loss diet but a healthy eating plan for life

This Diet Is Best for: Anyone who wants to be as well informed as they can about what they put on their plate. This is a diet plan that could benefit anyone of any age, and it will certainly help people over 50 fend off debilitating, age-related diseases. This is a detailed, practical guide to good nutrition.

Who Should Not Try This Diet: Those who are looking for a "secret formula" for quick weight loss or for promises of extended life and extraordinary fitness

reveal their weaknesses. One of the reasons the book is so long is that it provides a comprehensive food table with the nutrient content of each food, plus discussions of everything, literally, from soup to nuts. The information tells dieters what's good (low fat, high-fiber, and most nutritious), what's bad (high fat, low-fiber, empty calories) and how you can plan your new diet to keep some of your favorite foods on your weight-loss menus.

The Rationale

While some diets focus on limiting carbohydrate intake, the Goors' plan focuses on limiting fat intake, especially saturated fat, since fat is the most concentrated source of calories in the diet and saturated fat is linked to heart disease. The diet plan has no gimmicks or hooks; it's a no-nonsense approach to good nutrition that has withstood the test of time. Fat intake is limited but not excessively restricted, and the diet even allows for an occasional high-fat splurge. The goal, say the Goors, is not to think of *Choose to Lose* as a diet but as an eating plan for life. Foods are clearly divided into groups according to how much of them you can eat. The diet also provides examples of "before" menus and then shows better "after" alternatives. Follow the guidelines of their plan, say the Goors, and over time you will adjust your taste buds to a

Calorie Quota
The basic diet in the sample menus provides about 2,300 calories a day, which would accommodate an average man or an active woman. But it also provides information on ways to reduce the calorie count to between 1,500 and 1,600 without sacrificing good nutrition.

lower fat diet without having to greatly restrict your food choices.

What's for Breakfast, Lunch, and Dinner?
The Goors' diet provides more information about specific foods than most other diets, and it gives a week's worth of sample menus and recipes. More than 250 of the book's pages are devoted to food tables that give the calorie, fat, and saturated fat content of foods. You'll find brief, informative sections on such foods as bread, potatoes, cereals, chicken, seafood, popcorn, and pretzels, just to name a few. A typical day's menus might include oatmeal and whole-wheat toast with jelly, cottage cheese, strawberries, and skim milk for breakfast; chickpeas, whole wheat pita, a tangerine, carrot sticks, and orange juice for lunch; tortilla soup, chicken, green beans, rice, squash, cauliflower, nonfat yogurt, and blueberries for dinner; and nonfat yogurt and popcorn for snacks during the day. Total calories: 2,300. Guidelines are provided for cutting calories to 1,500 to 1,600—the minimum they recommend. Supplements are not recommended. Follow a balanced diet, they say, and

supplements shouldn't be necessary.

Fact or Fiction: What the Experts Say

Information is power, and the Goors' plan provides dieters with power over their diets and, ultimately, their health. The diet plan goes hand-in-hand with what most experts currently recommend, and it basically follows the USDA Food Guide Pyramid and meets the needs of seniors as well. It's a diet high in complex carbohydrates—mostly from whole grains, fruits, vegetables, and legumes—with limited fat intake, most of it from healthy fats such as olive oil. Though it's not billed as such, the diet is in line with dietary recommendations for reducing the risk of heart disease, diabetes, high blood pressure, and cancer.

Gains and Losses/ What's the Damage?

If you follow the Goors' plan, using the recommended calorie adjustments, it should allow you to lose weight successfully. You get a lot of variety and choices on this diet, which also offers much-needed guidance for keeping the diet balanced and realistic. One chapter is devoted to exercise, which they sum up as "Eating Right + Exercise = Perfection."

YES-YES'S
Fruits, vegetables, whole grains, variety, patience

NO-NO'S
High fat foods, especially foods rich in saturated fats; junk foods; fast foods; absentminded snacking

Other Similar Diets
Richard Simmons, Weight Watchers

Dieting With the Duchess

The Premise

Sarah Ferguson, Duchess of York, has been a spokesperson for Weight Watchers for years. Now she has a diet book that integrates much of the Weight Watchers diet program with her own philosophy about weight loss and maintenance. The diet is based on the premise that all calories count. No one type of calorie counts more or less than another. However, the diet counts points not calories, in keeping with the Weight Watchers program. In Weight Watchers, foods are given point values and you are allowed a maximum number of points each day. The Duchess emphasizes self-esteem and body image, and

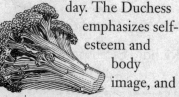

she lays out a no-nonsense eating and lifestyle plan that incorporates exercise. In fact, the Duchess' plan emphasizes physical activity more than most other plans.

The Rationale

Like Weight Watchers—which is what this diet plan actually is—the diet tries to be realistic and accommodating while encouraging slow dietary changes. The diet is designed to help you cut back on foods high in fat and sugar, but nothing is actually forbidden. A quick quiz helps you assess your current diet and how much you need to improve it. Dieting traps are considered a real problem for people trying to lose weight, so the Duchess gives several potentially disastrous scenarios along with a plan of action for each. Regular exercise is encouraged not just because it helps with weight loss but because it will give you a healthier, longer, and better quality life by boosting your immune system, lifting your mood, reducing your cancer risk, heating up your sex life, preventing osteoporosis, improving sleep, reducing your risk of heart disease, improving your memory, and enhancing your body image. There's even a guide to help you discover your personal exercise style and a separate chapter on how to fit exercise into your busy life.

Calorie Quota

The diet uses the point system, as does the Weight Watchers program, and no calorie counts are provided, though the diet is low in calories.

What's for Breakfast, Lunch, and Dinner?

Four weeks of menus are provided, and Weight Watchers planned points are pro-

This Diet Is Best for: Those who want to make some healthy changes in their diet and lose weight and who are willing to devote some extra time to planning, shopping, and preparing food, as well as exercising regularly

Who Should Not Try This Diet: People who have unusually low or unusually high calorie needs and those who are not willing and able to devote a considerable amount of time to food preparation

vided for each food, each meal, and each day. Depending on how much you weigh in the beginning, you are allotted anywhere from 18 to 35 points a day. Each food has a point value. For example, one cup of grapes is one point, and one slice of pizza is nine points. The higher the point value of a single food, the fewer the points left over for the rest of the day. The book includes about 80 recipes for foods in the four-week plan. The meals are varied and allow for small indulgences. However, as presented in the book, the diet requires a lot of food preparation. A typical day's menus include breakfast brushcetta and orange juice in the morning; leek and potato soup, a mini crudite platter with dipping sauce, herb-crusted grilled chicken breast, and fat-free milk for lunch; and citrus-seared tuna, mango salsa, green beans, and couscous for dinner. A snack might be a carton of low fat, artificially sweetened yogurt with fresh strawberries.

Quick Take

- A balanced, reduced-calorie plan emphasizing fruits, vegetables, and whole grains
- Emphasizes regular physical activity for weight loss
- Maintains that self-esteem and a good body image are critical to long-term success
- Expected weight loss is about two pounds per week

Fact or Fiction: What the Experts Say

Just about every nutritionist believes in the Weight Watchers diet program. However, the Duchess' program falls short by not providing a way to individualize the program either for points or calories. Point value lists are given only for the prepared dishes, not for individual foods in the menus or for any other foods, making it diffcult to plan your own meals or dine out. This separates the Duchess' diet from the original Weight Watchers

NO-NO'S

Inactivity, sugar, fatty meats, whole-fat dairy products

YES-YES'S

Positive attitude, lean meats, lots of fruits and vegetables, fat-free dairy products, lots of water, high-fiber foods, regular activity

plan, which came with detailed lists showing the point values for hundreds of foods. However, the Duchess' diet plan does get an "A" for its emphasis on physical activity.

Gains and Losses/ What's the Damage?

The diet is designed for a gradual weight loss of up to two pounds per week. Unlike the Weight Watchers program, it appears to be a one-size-fits-all diet. There are no guidelines for adjusting calorie intake or for making menu substitutions in the menus provided. The menus simply provide a certain number of calories, regardless of your build, your activity level, or your metabolism. The diet is obviously lower in fat and calories than a typical diet, with lots of healthy low fat, high-fiber foods (good for the over-50 crowd trying to fend off heart disease, diabetes, and constipation), so it should result in weight loss for most people. But it doesn't make allowances for people whose calorie requirements might be unusually high or unusually low.

Other Similar Diets

Nutri/System, Richard Simmons, Volumetrics, Weight Watchers

STICK-TO-IT-ABILITY RATING: 1 2 3 **4** 5

Eat, Drink, and Be Healthy

The Premise

Dr. Walter Willett, a well-known Harvard researcher, believes that the Food Guide Pyramid developed by the U.S. Department of Agriculture (USDA) is not only wrong, it's dangerous to your health. In its place he offers his own new and improved pyramid that focuses more on plant foods and de-emphasizes dairy. He even incorporates daily exercise and weight control into the pyramid. Willett falls somewhere between the pro-dairy and the anti-dairy camps that are duking it out these days. He's not totally against dairy products but doesn't believe there's a "calcium crisis," as many experts do. In fact, he says that drinking too much milk can actually make your body lose calcium because milk is high in protein, which causes the body to excrete calcium. He advocates getting calcium from other food sources and from supplements, if necessary. Other than that bit of controversy, Willett's diet offers up a healthy dose of good nutrition that's free of gimmicks and exaggerated promises. While the overall theme of the book is good nutrition, Willett calls weight control the number one nutritional factor for good health.

The Rationale

Control your weight, eat a plant-based diet with lots of

fruits, vegetables, and whole grains, limit dairy foods, exercise every day, and take a multivitamin for insurance: That's pretty much Willett's philosophy in a nutshell. He also says that drinking alcohol in moderation is probably healthy for most people, though he doesn't advise people to start drinking if they don't already. To back up his diet advice, he cites a lot of studies (he's been involved in much of the research himself) that suggest that these dietary changes are a boon to your health, reducing the risk of heart disease, cancer, diabetes, and stroke. By eating a plant-based diet, Willett points out that you increase your intake of phytonutrients, many of which are antioxidants that prevent disease-causing damage to the body's cells. It's not about deprivation or counting calories; it's about eating more of the right foods and much, much less of the wrong ones. While many diets

Calorie Quota

The sample menus and recipes provided in the book are based on a diet of 2,000 calories a day and include suggested adjustments to cut back to 1,600 calories a day for weight loss.

This Diet Is Best for: Anyone who is willing to make the switch to a mostly plant-based diet, cut out most rich indulgences, and exercise daily

Who Should Not Try This Diet: Anyone looking for a short-term weight loss program. This diet requires a commitment to long-term changes that ultimately will lead to better health.

admonish people to avoid foods with a high glycemic index (foods that cause a sudden rise in blood sugar), *Eat, Drink, and Be Healthy* offers a slightly modified version, called the glycemic load, that factors in a food's carbohydrate content, which Willett says is a more accurate representation of the impact specific foods have on blood sugar levels.

Quick Take

- A plant-based diet with lots of fruits, vegetables, and whole grains

- Makes physical activity and weight control an integral part of the diet

- Dairy products are not considered an essential part of the diet

- Glycemic load, rather than glycemic index, dictates which foods should be included

---

What's for Breakfast, Lunch, and Dinner?

Though there is no strict diet plan per se, the book provides a week's worth of sample menus and about 50 recipes in keeping with Willett's pyramid. But you're pretty much on your own in devising your menus and tracking your calorie intake. A typical day's menu might include fresh-squeezed orange juice and multigrain hotcakes for breakfast; grilled chicken, salad, cantaloupe, and strawberries for lunch; and mushroom meat loaf, roasted vegetables, green salad, and a spiced poached pear for dinner. Some of the sample menus have made allowances for a snack, and one even lays out the day's intake over six small meals. Coffee is allowed but sugar is not. A few sweet treats such as orange juice sorbet and rum-glazed pineapple are allowed, but there is no allowance for an occasional indulgence in fudge ice cream or cheesecake.

NO-NO'S	YES-YES'S
Following the USDA Food Guide Pyramid, eating lots of animal products such as beef and dairy, inactivity and being overweight, foods with a high glycemic load such as rice, white bread, potatoes, pasta, and sweets	Following Willett's own plant-based Healthy Eating Pyramid; eating lots of fruits, vegetables, legumes, and whole grains; exercising daily; controlling your weight; moderate alcohol intake if you already drink

Fact or Fiction: What the Experts Say

Though Willett's advice about dairy foods is controversial and his diet won't provide the amount of calcium currently recommended for folks over 50, the rest of his philosophy about how you should eat and control your weight is sound. He lays out a nutritious plan that will improve your health over the long term and fend off chronic diseases, such as diabetes, high blood pressure, and heart disease, which become increasingly common with age.

Gains and Losses/ What's the Damage?

Eat, Drink, and Be Healthy is not a plan for rapid weight loss. It's a diet designed to help you change your eating habits for good and improve your health. However, if you follow Willett's guidelines and adjust your calorie intake for weight control, you should lose weight while reaping the health benefits he promises.

Other Similar Diets

The Origin Diet; Eat More, Weigh Less

Eat More, Weigh Less

The Premise

Dr. Dean Ornish is famous for his strict low fat diet program that reduces heart disease risk and even reverses arterial damage. The findings from his now famous "Lifestyle Heart Trial" research, which show that major lifestyle changes can significantly reduce the risk of developing atherosclerosis and heart disease, are so well accepted that participation in one of the lifestyle program's hospital sites is even covered by some health insurance companies. His program restricts fat intake to ten percent or less of daily calories

This Diet Is Best for: People who are ready and willing to overhaul their lifestyle and eating habits and to sacrifice some of the pleasures of eating. Following the diet may only be possible if your whole family is up to the challenge.

Who Should Not Try This Diet: If you have trouble adjusting to change, then this diet is not for you. If you're into convenience foods and aren't willing to spend time preparing special low fat dishes, don't choose this diet.

and prohibits animal products, oils, and sugar. The Ornish plan calls for eating a very low fat vegetarian diet, relaxation, and exercise. A side benefit of the program, he discovered, is weight loss. How much the diet benefits you is not a matter of age but how well you follow the program. This book is already a classic; it was one of the first to advocate such a major cutback in fat while increasing the intake of complex carbohydrate foods. Here Ornish translates the Lifestyle Heart Trial program for people focusing on weight loss.

The Rationale

Ornish believes that it's better to make broad, comprehensive changes in your diet all at once rather than to make small, moderate changes. Thus, he advocates dropping your fat intake from the typical 30 to 40 percent of calories to 10 percent and switching from a diet high in sugar to one that contains virtually none. The rationale for the drastic reduction in fat, Ornish says, is that fat calories are more easily converted to fat in the body. A diet high in complex carbohydrates, on the other hand, is inefficient at converting the calories to fat. In fact, some calories are wasted during the conversion, allowing you to eat more calories than you could on a higher fat diet. Moreover, a diet low in fat is by default

---

Quick Take

- A very low fat diet (10 percent of total calories)

- Includes lots of fruits, vegetables, whole grains, and legumes

- Prohibits sweeteners and refined carbohydrates

- Requires meal preparation to ensure variety in the diet

- Encourages meditation and exercise

low in calories and reduces the body's production of free radicals, which are destructive compounds that are believed to contribute to the aging process.

What's for Breakfast, Lunch, and Dinner?

Eat More, Weigh Less provides more recipes than most diet books—and with good reason. It's tough to buy and prepare foods with such a low fat content. In fact, more than half the book's pages are devoted to recipes. A typical day's menu might include Scrambled Mexican Tofu, salsa, whole-wheat toast, and orange juice for breakfast; Black Pepper Polenta with Bell Pepper Sauce and Shiitake Mushrooms, Italian Bean Salad, Tossed Green Salad, and Melon Sorbet for lunch; Roasted Tomato Sandwiches, Anasazi Bean Soup with Corn and Chili, Oven-Roasted Potatoes with Fresh Herbs, green salad, fresh fruit, and Apples and Raspberries in Apple-Ginger Consommé for dinner. A table of some common foods and their nutrient content is also provided at the end of the book.

Fact or Fiction: What the Experts Say

Most experts acknowledge Ornish's body of research showing the dramatic opening of clogged arteries experienced by most people following his program. However, the biggest problem most experts have with Ornish's diet is that it's just not realistic for most people. The

Calorie Quota

There is no calorie quota and no food exchanges or allowances. The focus is on the type of calories, not the number. Generally speaking, it's rather difficult to overeat on a diet that contains only ten percent calories from fat.

real test of any diet program is how easy it is to stick with over the long haul. Regardless of how healthful a diet may be, it's useless if you can't stay on it.

YES-YES'S
Fruits, vegetables, whole grains, legumes, meditation, exercise

That lack of stick-to-it-ability may be the downfall of Ornish's plan for the majority of people.

NO-NO'S
Fatty foods, oils, sugar, sweeteners, refined grains

Gains and Losses/What's the Damage?

There's no doubt that if you're able to stick with it, Ornish's diet works. The question is whether you're willing to go that far with your dietary changes. Though exercise is encouraged, especially walking, few specifics are provided about how to get started and keep going. And because the diet is so low in fat, you'll need to do some special food preparation every day if you want to avoid meal monotony. While the diet should help lower your risk of cardio-vascular disease, it could be low in some fat-soluble vitamins that are so important as you age, such as vitamins D and E, if you don't supplement them. The same is true of calcium. While calcium-rich, fat-free dairy products are allowed on the diet, the sample menus provide only about one serving a day—not nearly enough to meet your increased calcium needs.

Other Similar Diets

The Pritikin Weight-Loss Breakthrough

Eat Right 4 Your Type

The Premise

This diet was developed by Dr. Peter D'Adamo, a naturopathic physician who maintains that your blood type is the key to weight gain as well as to health, disease, longevity, vitality, emotional strength, and personality. According to D'Adamo, your blood type (O, A, B, or AB) is a part of your biological heritage. Each blood type handles food differently and, therefore, requires a different diet. Type O's, for instance, are descended from hunters and must be meat eaters to maintain optimum health and to lose weight. Type A's, on the other hand, are vegetarians. Eating foods incompatible with your blood type poses considerable health risks according to this theory. But if you stick with the com-

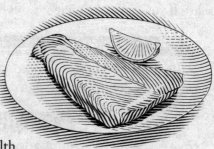

plicated do's and don'ts of the different blood type diets, you are supposed to be able to fight off viruses and infections, rid the body of toxins, and even prevent cancer, cardiovascular disease, and diabetes. This diet is promoted for overall good health, with weight loss as a side benefit. D'Adamo also claims to have discovered a critical link between blood type and aging. By following the diet, he says, you will absorb nutrients as well as you did when you were younger and slow down the aging process during your entire adult life.

This Diet Is Best for: No one. There's no scientific evidence to support the diet's premise, so there's no reason for anyone to subject themselves to the dietary acrobatics required to follow it. And, despite its reputation as a weight-loss diet, it's not designed for people to lose weight.

Who Should Not Try This Diet: No one should try this diet. It's a waste of time and likely to be extremely frustrating.

The Rationale

According to D'Adamo, certain foods contain compounds called lectins that, if incompatible with your blood type, deposit themselves in tissues and damage them. Eat a food containing lectins that are incompatible with your blood type, he says, and they will target organs and cause blood cells to clump together. D'Adamo claims that weight loss is a natural side effect of following the appropriate blood type diet. In addition, he says that incompatible lectins interfere with the production of insulin and upset the body's hormonal balance, which in turn causes weight gain. D'Adamo claims to have tested virtually all common foods for blood

Calorie Quota
There is no limit on calorie intake. However, serving sizes sometimes vary according to the dieter's ethnicity and there tends to be a range to choose from. If you opt for the smaller servings, you'll probably lose weight.

type reactions; his findings are the basis for the diet.

What's for Breakfast, Lunch, and Dinner?

The menus vary greatly, depending upon your blood type. For example, Type O's are supposed to eat a lot of meat, but dairy products are all but forbidden. You would need to carry the book with you at all times in order to follow the plan with accuracy. For example, Type B's can have salmon but not sea bass. Type O's are allowed blueberries but not blackberries. And the lists go on...and on...and on. It gets even more complicated with further breakdowns into separate diet lists for Type B's who are of Asian descent and Type O's of African ancestry.

> ## Quick Take
>
> - Meal plans are based on the four basic blood types
> - Diet plans can range from vegetarian to one that encourages a lot of meat consumption, depending on your blood type
> - No calorie limits but a lot of forbidden foods
> - Complex and confusing lists of foods that are allowed and forbidden, depending on blood type and ethnic background

Fact or Fiction: What the Experts Say

D'Adamo provides complicated and detailed biologic explanations for the blood type connection. These explanations sound impressive but have little basis in fact. Timothy Gorski, M.D., associate editor for the *Scientific Review of Alternative Medicine*, says it's a cutesy theory that's more fiction than fact. He points out that AB blood typing is only one system for identifying blood types. There are many other blood factors that make each person's blood profile unique, which are not taken into consideration. Other doctors take exception to the idea that lectin proteins in food cause the blood to clump in people who are not genetically suited to consume it. They say that this kind of blood coagulation is so serious and life threatening that if this were a common phenomenon, scientists and doctors would be well aware of it. And, they say, D'Adamo has presented no photographic evidence of the difference between muscle fibers in people who are eating a diet that is "correct" for their blood type and people who are not.

NO-NO'S
Depends on your blood type

YES-YES'S
Depends on your blood type

Gains and Losses/ What's the Damage?

The diet planning is so difficult, it's tough to determine if someone would actually lose weight. D'Adamo barely addresses exercise, and again, different suggestions are made depending on blood type. Planning around the dietary do's and don'ts becomes an almost impossible task in a family, where more than one blood type is likely to coexist. You also could end up consuming less-than-adequate amounts of some nutrients and overconsuming others, depending on which diet type you follow.

Other Similar Diets
None

Eat Right, Live Longer

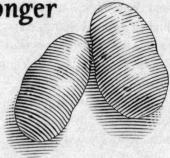

The Premise

This diet book, written by Dr. Neil Barnard, president of the Physicians' Committee for Responsible Medicine, promises to unleash the power of foods to improve your health and delay the aging process. Barnard advocates a low fat vegetarian diet, and he focuses on dietary changes that he says will protect cells from disease, clean the blood, boost immunity, and balance hormones. His diet will also help you avoid contaminants in food, such as hormones, pesticides,

and chlorine, that make you sick. Weight loss is not the primary goal of Barnard's diet; in fact, only one chapter in the book is actually devoted to it. But when it comes to losing weight, Barnard says that the most powerful weight-control menu is a vegetarian one. If you follow his plan for good eating, he says you can forget diets forever and eat normal portions at every meal.

The Rationale

Barnard's vegetarian diet prescription has a lot to do with maintaining good health and little to do with weight loss. He advocates avoiding meat and dairy because they are loaded with chemicals, hormones, and drugs that can weaken our immune systems and make us sick. He bases his high-carbohydrate diet for weight loss on research showing that calories from carbohydrates are inefficiently converted to fat by the body and, during their conversion to body fat, burn more energy than fat calories. He also points to research showing that people produce more body heat after a high-carbohydrate meal, indicating that they burn calories faster. He even refers to high-carbohydrate foods as foods with a negative calorie effect. Moreover, he says that foods can have a dramatic effect on hormones, which can affect weight loss and overall health. The goal is to keep hormones from surging. Too much fat in the diet causes hormones to increase, while fiber helps to lower hormone levels.

Calorie Quota

The diet recommends not to drop calorie intake below 10 calories per pound of your ideal weight. For example, if you're aiming for 135 pounds, don't go below 1,350. No other calorie guidelines are provided.

This Diet Is Best for: People who have been considering a vegetarian diet and would like to lose weight. It's also best for people who are willing to spend more preparation time in the kitchen. Few allowances are made for convenience foods.

Who Should Not Try This Diet: People who love milk, meat, or cheese or who prefer more information to allow flexibility at mealtime

What's for Breakfast, Lunch, and Dinner?

This book contains about 100 pages devoted to recipes, two weeks' worth of menus primarily based on those recipes, shopping tips, and a guide to equipping your kitchen for low fat vegetarian cooking. A typical day might include applesauce muffins, fruit preserves, and an apricot smoothie for breakfast; curried lentil soup, potatoes, spinach salad, and fruit salad for lunch; and pasta with broccoli and fresh tomatoes, garlic bread, mixed green salad with fat-free dressing, and fresh apricot crisp for dinner. Barnard pushes a "Zero-A-Day" program for meats and dairy products. He also encourages eating raw fruits and vegetables to boost

---

Quick Take

- A low fat vegetarian diet to boost immunity, balance hormones, and protect cells from damage

- Encourages eating only organic produce to avoid pesticides

- Includes raw fruits and vegetables to boost antioxidant levels

---

the body's production of glutathione, an antioxidant compound that "hauls toxins out of the body." While the diet discourages sugar intake, it does not focus on the glycemic index of foods (the degree to which a food raises blood sugar levels) as many other diets do.

Fact or Fiction: What the Experts Say

The diet is a healthy one, but it would be difficult to follow for people not committed to vegetarianism. The two biggest concerns about people over 50 following this diet, experts say, is the lack of vitamins B_{12} and D and the mineral calcium. The diet does provide tips for getting B_{12}, aside from a multivitamin, but the need for calcium and vitamin D are seriously down-played. Barnard's philosophy is that if you follow this type of diet, you don't need as much

NO-NO'S

Meat, dairy, caffeine, nonorganic produce, tap water (because of its chlorine content)

calcium to maintain healthy bones because it's lower in calcium-depleting protein. And he says that just a little sun exposure will be enough to trigger vitamin D production in your skin. But that doesn't take into account the fact that your body's ability to produce vitamin D diminishes with age as the requirement for the vitamin goes up.

And if you follow it to the letter, you should lose weight. The diet should also decrease your risk of developing diabetes, heart disease, hypertension, and possibly cancer. However, following it depends on your commitment to giving up meat and

YES-YES'S

Lots of fruits, vegetables, and whole grains; organic produce; bottled water

dairy and your willingness to spend more money on organic foods and more time in the kitchen. If you decide to go for it, keep a watch on your intake of vitamin B_{12}, calcium, and vitamin D.

Gains and Losses/What's the Damage?

Overall, this is a healthy vegetarian diet.

Other Similar Diets

Eat More,
Weigh Less

Eating Well for Optimum Health

The Premise

Dr. Andrew Weil is a well-known guru of alternative medicine and the author of several books on health and nutrition. This diet guide ties together his philosophy about lifestyle, nutrition, and well-being. His "eating well" program is designed not just to keep you fit and healthy but also to satisfy your senses, giving you pleasure and comfort. Austerity is not a part of his plan.

Weil presents his eating-well plan as one strategy for managing disease and restoring health. Much of the book is devoted to providing good, basic nutrition information, and only one chapter is devoted to weight loss. But weight loss or weight maintenance are not Weil's primary goals here. Instead, he focuses on eating a variety of healthy foods and adopting a healthy lifestyle.

This Diet Is Best for: Anyone who wants to be gently guided into a new way of eating healthfully that makes mealtime a slow-paced, enjoyable experience. The diet is well-balanced and is well-suited to anyone of any age who wants to feel their best.

Who Should Not Try This Diet: There really are no caveats against following Weil's Eating Well plan.

The Rationale

Weil says that by embracing and enjoying the eating experience rather than trying to subdue and deny it, you'll find it easier to make wise food choices that can improve your quality of life for years to come. His message on diet and health seems to be that you should delight in eating, choose foods wisely, exercise, and be happy. The diet is one that follows almost all of the tenets currently accepted as the nutrition path to good health, including eating less refined and processed food, avoiding foods containing partially hydrogenated oils, including soybeans and soy foods in your diet, eating fish at least two to three times a week, keeping your protein intake between 10 and 20 percent of your caloric intake, reducing your consumption of red meat; eating beans, legumes, and whole grains; and eating lots of fruits and vegetables.

> ### Calorie Quota
> Calories are not counted, and there are no specific meal plans. You should lose weight, though, if you follow Weil's advice on which foods to avoid and which ones to eat more of.

What's for Breakfast, Lunch, and Dinner?

Though there are no menus nor a strict diet plan to follow (only eating guidelines and recipes), Weil recommends that your daily diet provide about 50 to 60 percent of calories from carbohydrates, 10 to 20 percent of calories from protein, and about 20 percent of calories from fat. If you drop below 20 percent of calories from fat, he says, you may develop a deficiency of essential fatty acids. Weil encourages a diet filled with high-fiber complex carbohydrates, and low glycemic-index foods (those that don't raise blood sugar much). He discourages sugary foods, foods sweetened with high fructose corn syrup, and products made with refined flour but says that many popular diet plans are overly concerned about sugar intake. The book provides several lists of foods and sample meals, but the mixing and matching and menu planning are up to you. He does, however, give about 80 tasty-sounding recipes. Weil doesn't come right out and recommend a complete vegetarian diet, but you won't find any meat- or egg-based dishes in the meal plans or recipes. He does suggest minimizing your intake of animal-based foods while increasing your intake of plant-based ones.

Fact or Fiction: What the Experts Say

Weil enjoys considerable respect from both conventional and alternative camps alike. His dietary advice, for the most part, is in line with what most mainstream health experts and nutritionists recommend. However, he does steer readers away from dairy products, which could make it tough to get all the calcium and vitamin D your bones need to stay strong. His recommendation for fiber intake is higher than most—about 40 grams a

Quick Take

- Based on the principle that eating should be an enjoyable as well as a healthy experience

- Primarily a vegetarian diet with lots of fruits, vegetables, and whole grains

- No specific calorie counts or meal plans

- Not a weight-loss plan per se but a diet plan to improve health

NO-NO'S

A lot of animal foods, such as meat, poultry, and dairy; inactivity; severe dietary restrictions; not enjoying meal time; high glycemic-index foods; overly processed foods, especially those that contain hydrogenated oils, which are high in trans fatty acids

YES-YES'S

Lots of fruits and vegetables; soy foods; foods rich in omega-3 fats; minimal amounts of dairy, eggs, meat, and poultry; plenty of fluids; leisurely meal times; satisfying hunger

your diet doesn't include all the foods in his healthy eating plan, he recommends a variety of supplements, including B vitamins, vitamin E, and

day—and could cause some stomach discomfort if you don't ease into it gradually.

Gains and Losses/ What's the Damage?

If you follow Weil's guidelines for eating well, you may not only lose weight and improve your health but actually allow yourself to enjoy your meals. If

selenium, to bridge the gap. In addition, it would be a good idea to take a calcium and vitamin D supplement as insurance against the increased loss of calcium from bones you experience as you age.

Other Similar Diets

Eat More, Weigh Less; Eat Right, Live Longer

Fight Fat Over Forty

The Premise

In this book, Dr. Pamela Peeke, an assistant clinical professor of medicine at the University of Maryland and an adjunct senior scientist at the National Institutes of Health, details how chronic stress contributes to weight gain and threatens the length and quality of life after the age of forty. Peeke sets out to bring women harmony of mind and body by working with and around hormonal changes that cause what she calls "toxic stress." Toxic stress triggers the release of stress hormones which, she says, leads to toxic weight gain. In fact, the average weight gain during the years preceding menopause (lasting five to ten years) can be two to three pounds or more per year. Part of that is due to a gradual decline in

This Diet Is Best for: Women who want to improve their diet and their physical fitness

Who Should Not Try This Diet: Women who are not willing to give up after-dinner munching

energy requirements. (Women older than 40 require about 15 percent less energy than they did in their 20's.) In addition, Peeke also points to the role daily hormonal fluctuations play in weight gain and identifies what she calls "The Cortizone," the period between 4 P.M. and 11 P.M. when levels of the hormone cortisol are lowest and you're most at risk for overeating and storing fat. She offers a variety of tips for navigating The Cortizone, including not eating carbohydrate foods after 5 P.M. and not eating at all after 8 P.M.

The Rationale

By controlling your diet—both what and when you eat—and making exercise a regular part of your lifestyle, Peeke says you can minimize weight gain and stay fit at midlife and beyond. In her plan, stress management, regular exercise, and physical fitness are as critical to weight management and weight loss as diet. Her fitness requirements for stress and weight management are not negotiable and include 45 minutes of exercise five or six days a week, whole body strength training at least twice a week, and daily stretching.

What's for Breakfast, Lunch, and Dinner?

According to Peeke, women are either stress resilient, stress overeaters, or stress undereaters. The diet plan for stress overeaters is designed for

---

Quick Take

- Geared toward women over 40

- Based on hormonal changes that occur during menopause

- Provides a balanced diet with lots of fruits, vegetables, and whole grains

- Emphasizes physical activity

weight loss. For the stress-resilient profile, she offers a basic healthy balanced diet. For the stress undereaters, she includes extras such as nutrition bars and shakes, granola, and nuts for extra calories. A typical day consists of cereal, fresh fruit, and skim milk for breakfast; a sandwich, carrot and celery sticks, fresh fruit, and skim milk for lunch; poultry or fish, two vegetables, and fresh fruit for dinner; and a mid-morning and mid-afternoon snack. Generally, each meal is made up of about 55 percent carbohydrates, 15 to 20 percent protein, and 25 to 30 percent fat. No matter which stress profile fits you, Peeke says your daily diet should include at least six servings of whole grains; six to eight servings of vegetables; five to six servings of fruits; two to three servings of low fat dairy; two servings of meat, poultry, fish, or beans; and two tablespoons of vegetable oils. All diets should include 20 to 35 grams of fiber a day and at least eight glasses of water. And everyone should minimize or avoid eating foods made from refined processed sugars.

Fact or Fiction: What the Experts Say

The diet itself is a healthy one that follows all the accepted healthy eating guidelines. What hasn't been proved, however, are the reasons behind her admonition to avoid eating carbohydrates after 5 P.M. and not to eat at all after 8 P.M. If you have a problem with out-of-control munching in the evening, then perhaps you should heed her advice. But there's no evidence to suggest that carbohydrates in particular or food in general

Calorie Quota

Though calories are not the focus, Peeke says her diet plans provide about 1,500 calories a day. She does not recommend going below 1,200 calories a day.

is more likely to turn to fat if you eat it after a certain hour. Peeke's insistence on physical activity to maintain health and control weight, however, is to be applauded.

NO-NO'S

High glycemic-index foods (foods that cause blood sugar levels to surge), fried foods, eating after 8 P.M., inactivity, stress

Gains and Losses/What's the Damage?

Following the balanced diet plan for 1,500 calories a day and including all the suggested servings of whole grains, fruits, vegetables, and low fat dairy should result in weight loss and provide all the nutrients you need, with the possible exception of calcium. The two to

three servings a day of dairy that Peeke recommends provide only about 600 to 900 milligrams (mg) of calcium, not sufficient for anyone, let alone postmenopausal women who need 1,200 to 1,500 mg a day. And since fortified milk is the only realistic dietary source for vitamin D,

YES-YES'S

Physical activity, stress reduction, a balanced diet including whole grains, fruits, vegetables, nonfat dairy, lean meats, reduced-fat cheeses

two to three glasses a day would also fall short of current recommendations.

Other Similar Diets

SugarBusters!

Fit for Life

The Premise

This 1985 diet book by Harvey and Marilyn Diamond has sold millions of copies over the years and continues to be a popular volume, despite more than 15 years of scathing criticism from health experts. There are two basic tenets of this food-combining weight-loss diet: 1. It's not what you eat but when you eat and how you combine your food that determines weight loss and health. 2. Always eat fruit alone, never just before, just after, or with other foods.

Though those two themes are constant throughout the book, the Diamonds give many more dietary rules that must be followed in order to lose weight and be healthy. The book generally follows the food combination teachings of Herbert M. Shelton, a naturopath who developed the Natural Hygiene diet. According to Shelton's theory, the body experiences three digestive cycles during the day: *appropriation,* which is eating and digesting (noon to 8 P.M.), *assimilation,* which is absorption and use of nutrients (8 P.M. to 4 A.M.), and *elimination* of body wastes (4 A.M. to noon). The Diamonds say that only by eating foods in the right combinations at the right times,

This Diet Is Best for: This diet is not recommended for anyone.

Who Should Not Try This Diet: This diet is not recommended for anyone..

following these natural cycles, can the body rid itself of toxins and excess weight. They also clearly suggest that following the program can fend off diseases related to aging, such as heart and kidney disease, stroke, diabetes, and other age-related conditions including balding and hearing loss.

The Rationale

The rationale behind *Fit for Life* is anything but rational. Among the nuggets of nutritional wisdom dispensed by the Diamonds are: Eating foods in the wrong combinations causes them to rot so they cannot be used by the body and they turn to fat; fruits and vegetables, because of their high water content, wash and cleanse the body of toxins, but if fruit is eaten at the end of a meal, it ferments and causes digestion and weight problems; all the nutrients the body needs are found in fruits and vegetables; eating combinations of foods, such as meat and potatoes or bread and cheese, causes obesity and disease; and toxic waste material is kept inside the body

Calorie Quota

Calories are not counted or restricted on the Diamond program. However, calorie intake is likely to be reduced because the emphasis is on fruits and vegetables, which are low in calories, and many foods are forbidden or severely restricted.

if there is not enough energy (through proper food combining) to excrete it. Improper food combining, they say, leads to many age-related diseases.

What's for Breakfast, Lunch, and Dinner?

If you follow the Diamonds' do's and don'ts, a typical day's menu calls for only fruit or fruit juice before noon, fruit and a salad for lunch, vegetables and either a starch or protein food for dinner, and fruit for a snack—but only if you wait at least three hours after dinner. Eggs and dairy products (except for unpasteurized butter, sour cream, whipping cream, white cheese, and yogurt) are all but forbidden. Simply put: Any food besides

fruits and vegetables is considered a "concentrated food" (having a low water content) and these cannot be combined with one another; fruit must be eaten on an empty stomach.

Fact or Fiction: What the Experts Say

Although Shelton died in 1985, the basics of his theories have been recycled and reinvented many times over by several diet book authors in addition to the Diamonds. Despite their broad appeal, these theories have been universally panned by experts as unscientific, ineffective, and potentially dangerous. That's because they dictate a nutritionally unbalanced diet, recommend eating unpasteur-

---

Quick Take

- Food-combining diet that dictates which foods should be eaten, in what combinations, and at which time of the day

- Based on the theory that eating foods in the "wrong" combinations causes weight gain and illness

- Deficient in several important nutrients

ized dairy products, and ignore potential negative physical reactions dieters might have to the eating plan. No scientific

NO-NO'S

Combining different types of food, such as proteins and carbohydrate foods, or combining fruit with any other foods; dairy products (except butter); sugar; cooked eggs

proof exists that this food-combining diet either prevents the buildup of harmful toxins or helps weight loss.

food-combining diet rids the body of fat-causing toxins. You lose weight on this diet because it's quite restrictive and low in calories. One analysis of the diet found it to be low in several nutrients that are important for seniors, including calcium, zinc, and vitamins B_{12} and D. Especially alarming is the fact that the Diamonds urge dieters to

YES-YES'S

Lots of fruits and vegetables (but only if eaten in the right combination with other foods)

Gains and Losses/ What's the Damage?

On the plus side, the Diamonds encourage dieters to eat lots of fruits and vegetables. Unfortunately, that's at the expense of other healthful foods. Though anyone who sticks with the Diamonds' program will likely lose weight, it's not because the

ignore signals that something could be wrong, such as diarrhea, dizziness, or headaches, which they attribute to the body ridding itself of toxins.

Other Similar Diets

Suzanne Somers' Eat, Cheat, and Melt the Fat Away

STICK-TO-IT-ABILITY RATING: 1 2 **3** 4 5

Jenny Craig

The Premise

The Jenny Craig program was founded more than 15 years ago by a woman named Jenny Craig who was struggling with her own weight. At the time, the program was unique because it offered frozen or shelf-stable prepared meals to help with portion management and calorie-intake control. Today Jenny Craig has 800 centers, making it one of the largest weight management programs in the world. Jenny Craig offers weekly one-on-one counseling that provides both information and motivation. Developed by registered dietitians and psychologists, the program focuses on lifestyle changes, such as incorporating

This Diet Is Best for: People who prefer total support and guidance over a more independent approach to dieting

Who Should Not Try This Diet: People with a limited budget or those who don't like being told what to eat. Also, Jenny Craig requires a time commitment for the weekly counseling sessions. If eating out is a big part of your work or your life, then this plan probably isn't the best choice.

exercise into your daily life, and diverting your attention from food. If you don't have a Jenny Craig Weight Loss Centre near you or if you prefer to go it alone, you can try Jenny Direct, the at-home program. Jenny Direct offers a personalized weight-loss program, delivery of materials to your home, and weekly support consultations over the phone.

The Rationale

With individual counseling and prepackaged meals, the program leaves little to chance—or to the dieter's discretion. Jenny Craig helps you set a realistic weight-loss goal and then helps you craft a plan to successfully achieve that goal. The program says it teaches you how to manage food, feelings, and fitness. Jenny Craig believes that the combination of complete

> ### Calorie Quota
> Calorie levels are calculated by computer for each individual at the start of the program. They can range from 1,000 to 2,300 calories a day.

support, step-by-step instruction about what to eat, and controlled portions during the initial dieting stage together help dieters win at weight loss.

What's for Breakfast, Lunch, and Dinner?

The diet consists of three meals and three snacks per day. About 20 percent of the daily calories are from protein, 20 percent from fat, and 60 percent from carbohydrates. During the initial phase, and as long as it takes to knock off the first half of the total number of pounds you want to lose, Jenny Craig requires that you purchase and eat Jenny Craig prepared entrées and snacks every day at every meal. There is a wide variety of dishes to choose from, including such options as sweet and sour chicken, beef sirloin dinner, pancakes and vegetarian sausage, and double chocolate cake. Written materials and your diet counselor will help you add fruits, vegetables, dairy foods, and whole grains to the Jenny Craig dishes. The number of calories you should consume every day is calculated according to your height and weight, but you are not allowed to go below a minimum of 1,000 calories. Diet plans are available for vegetarians, people with diabetes, and those who observe kosher dietary laws.

Once the first half of your extra weight is lost, you can begin the transition to supermarket food, using a food diary to keep a record of everything you eat. Counselors guide dieters with their new food choices, and the dieter and counselor together decide how rapidly or how slowly the transition to supermarket foods should be made.

Fact or Fiction: What the Experts Say

If you follow the prescribed diet, you'll eat a balanced, nutritious, reduced-calorie diet. However, like most commercial weight-loss programs, there is no research to show that Jenny Craig's program is effective over the long haul. "It may be a good way to get started, but for the dieter, very little thought is going into what they're doing in the beginning. The dieter has no

---

Quick Take

- Offers a variety of prepared, packaged meals and snacks that are required during the initial phase of dieting

- Safe and nutritionally balanced

- Requires weekly, one-on-one counseling sessions

- Encourages gradual weight loss

- Can be expensive

control over what they're eating," says Liz Ward, M.S., R.D., nutrition counselor in Reading, Massachusetts. And, while the counselors are

NO-NO'S

Anything except what's on preplanned menus, eating out

YES-YES'S

Jenny Craig prepared entrées and snacks; prescribed amounts of fruits, vegetables, dairy products, and whole grains

trained to be Jenny Craig counselors, they are not nutritionists. Keep in mind that it's almost impossible to get all the nutrients you need from 1,000 calories a day. It's healthier if you set 1,200 or 1,500 calories as your personal minimum calorie intake.

as recommended, you can expect to lose one to two pounds a week. Though the diet is a safe and healthy one for any age, it doesn't come cheap. Prices vary depending on your individual choices, but the company says the average cost is about $65 a week, including entrées and snacks. There are generally three membership options. Depending on which membership level and which meals and snacks you choose, it can cost you about $400 during the first month of the program.

Gains and Losses/What's the Damage?

If you follow the program (no cheating) and exercise

Other Similar Diets

Nutri/System, Weight Watchers

Low-Fat Lies, High-Fat Frauds

The Premise

This diet book, written by a physician and a nutritionist team from Brown University, espouses neither a low fat diet nor a low-carbohydrate diet. In fact, it's not really a diet book, if by "diet" you mean a weight-loss plan. Rather, *Low-Fat Lies, High-Fat Frauds* is a book about healthy eating, with weight loss as a side benefit. Kevin Vigilante, clinical associate professor of medicine at Brown, and co-author Mary Flynn, a nutritionist and Brown faculty member, advocate the Mediterranean style of eating, a diet that is rich in olive oil, fish, vegetables, fruits, beans, and lentils and includes a daily glass or two of red wine. Research confirms that the Mediterranean diet lowers cholesterol and reduces the risk of cancer, and this book explains why and how. In addition, the authors

This Diet Is Best for: People who like vegetables and whole grains and feel they would benefit from the more liberal dietary guidelines the authors advocate

Who Should Not Try This Diet: Those who have a problem with alcohol and those who feel they need more specific dietary guidelines

"expose the failures, false promises, and potential dangers of low fat diets," as well as those of the popular high fat (and low-carbohydrate) diets. Vigilante and Flynn also acknowledge the importance of exercise but say you can get the exercise you need to lose weight and stay healthy without becoming a "gym rat." The authors point out that some of the largest consumers of olive oil, such as people who live in Spain, are also among those with the longest life spans. Moreover, the diet promises to help prevent killer diseases such as heart disease and diabetes, which become so much more common with age.

> ### Calorie Quota
> There is no set calorie limit. Sample menus are provided for 1,500- and 2,000-calorie diets.

The Rationale

Research has shown that the traditional Mediterranean diet has, for thousands of years, resulted in some of the lowest rates of heart disease, cancer, and diabetes in the world. Much of the research is discussed in the book, which has an impressive 300 references. The authors disagree with the official diets of the American Heart Association and the National Institutes of Health, which recommend limiting fat intake to 30 percent of calories. Rather, they say that cutting back on fat can backfire, leaving you hungry and with a high level of risky fats in your blood. The Mediterranean diet provides about 40 percent of calories from fat, primarily from olive oil, which has heart-healthy properties. They maintain, and provide the science to explain, that the right kind of fat actually helps you stay healthy and lose weight.

What's for Breakfast, Lunch, and Dinner?

The book provides a week's worth of menus for a 1,500-

calorie and a 2,000-calorie diet, along with about 75 recipes for healthy dishes that fit the Mediterranean eating style. The diet includes lots of fruits, vegetables, whole grains, fish, and olive oil. Four tablespoons of olive oil are allowed on the 1,500-calorie-a-day diet while 6 tablespoons are allowed on the 2,000-calorie-a-day diet, which doesn't leave a lot of room for "cheats." The diets provided aren't prescriptive for weight loss; the authors advise that you simply eat fewer calories if you don't lose weight. Because of its heart-protective properties, a glass or two of red wine a day is included in the Mediterranean diet. It's unclear whether the calories from the wine are included in the two diets, as the sample menus don't list wine, but throughout the book the authors recommend that one should drink it. For more specifics on the diet, check out the Web site at www.meddiet.com.

Quick Take

- A healthy diet modeled after the traditional diets of people in Mediterranean countries

- Higher in fat than most diets, with much of the fat coming from olive oil

- Includes lots of fruits, vegetables, beans, lentils, fruit, and whole grains

- Recommends drinking one to two glasses of red wine a day

Fact or Fiction: What the Experts Say

The American Heart Association cautiously acknowledges that the incidence of heart disease in Mediterranean countries is lower than in the United States. But it points out that other lifestyle factors may play just as important a role in reducing risk. While some experts have researched the Mediterranean diet and are advocates of it, others believe the diet is an open invitation to overeat.

YES-YES'S
Olive oil, red wine, vegetables, beans, lentils, fruit

Gains and Losses/ What's the Damage?

The Mediterranean-style diet the authors promote is generally an excellent one that incorporates all the foods that nutrition experts say we should eat more of. And it also advises cutting back on foods we eat too much of, such as meat, processed foods, and high fat junk. Some experts fear that the diet is too liberal and can easily result in eating too many calories because of the higher fat content. And several experts have a problem with the recommendation to drink a glass or two of red wine each day, fearing it could

open the door to drinking problems. If you currently take any medication, be sure to check with your doctor about any potential interactions. You may also fall short of

NO-NO'S
Reduced-fat foods, hydrogenated fats, and foods high in saturated fat, such as red meat and full-fat dairy products

calcium and vitamin D since the authors don't emphasize low fat dairy products or supplements, putting you at increased risk for osteoporosis. However, the authors claim that because the diet isn't high in protein, which leeches calcium out of the body, less calcium is needed to maintain healthy bones.

Other Similar Diets
The Origin Diet

Making the Case for Yourself: A Diet Book for Smart Women

The Premise

Susan Estrich, a prominent lawyer and frequent CNN legal commentator, uses her impressive legal skills to build a case for dieting. And her arguments are compelling and motivational. She doesn't target a specific age group, only a specific gender: women. According to Estrich, a woman's brain is her secret dieting weapon. She urges women to think positively, to use logic when face-to-face with a 600-calorie blueberry muffin (no matter how lousy your day has been, the muffin will only make it worse, and it's probably stale anyway), and to take responsibility for their actions. Estrich, who used to be overweight herself, says that it was a profound attitude change, not a particular dieting gimmick, that allowed her to finally lose weight and keep it off. She made a commitment to herself—a contract, if you will—and she didn't break it. She came up with a plan for keeping her commitment, and she constantly reminded herself about what she was doing and why she was doing it. Using her own experience, Estrich shows readers how to do the same for themselves.

The Rationale

Estrich approaches dieting as a lawyer approaches a case. It's not the specific rules of law that are most important, she says, but rather the arguments one uses that make or break a case—or your diet. So Estrich helps you build the case for yourself so you can stick with your weight-loss efforts. She shows you how to resist whatever food is calling out to you by anticipating temptation and being ready with logical arguments against them. Estrich maintains that following impulses and emotions, becoming stupid about our bodies, is what ultimately blows a diet. You have two choices, she says: You can decide that losing weight is important and make space for it in your life or you can decide it's not important. Once you've made up your mind to do it, she offers dieters a three-week contract to sign. The three-week commitment is crucial because that's how long it takes to really alter your

> ## Quick Take
>
> - A motivational, self-help book for women who want to lose weight and keep it off
>
> - Emphasizes making a contract with yourself to lose weight
>
> - Guidelines for how to face reality and take responsibility for what you eat

---

This Diet Is Best for: Women who want to be independent, motivated, and strong and just need an extra push in the right direction

Who Should Not Try This Diet: Women who feel they just can't go it alone and need the support that weekly meetings and expert counseling provide; this is a do-it-yourself dieting approach

eating behavior. To start you off, Estrich then provides four diets (although they're pretty loose as diets go) for you to follow during those first three weeks.

What's for Breakfast, Lunch, and Dinner?

Estrich's four-phase miracle diet is actually a blend of some popular diet plans. The purpose of following the diet for three weeks is to take advantage of your early enthusiasm for dieting, to provide you with early weight-loss success, and to show you that you have power over food. She starts with a modified cabbage soup diet for the first three days, then provides different basic meal plans for various periods of time. Estrich doesn't provide specific quantities of food but does tell you what kinds of food to eat, concentrating on vegetables, fruit, and lean protein. A few recipes

are included at the back of the book. Along with general guidelines, Estrich offers a steady diet of no-nonsense motivation. She knows what your weakness will be and where diets fail, and she prepares you to deal with those. And she provides a list of foods you can eat that contain 100 calories.

Fact or Fiction: What the Experts Say

Estrich's book hasn't received as much attention as the more outrageous diets. But it's worth serious consideration. However, at least one weight-loss expert says that while it may be just right for some women, it may not be enough for others. "While she offers very good strategies for anyone who wants to alter their current eating habits, there may be people who find they need help from someone else in order to help make that

Calorie Quota
Because there is no diet plan or food exchange lists, there is no calorie limit.

happen," says Cindy Moore, M.S., R.D. director of nutrition therapy at the Cleveland Clinic Foundation and a spokesperson for the American

NO-NO'S
Fad diets, placing blame, excuses

Dietetic Association. "However, it might very well act as a supplement to more specific nutrition guidance."

Gains and Losses/ What's the Damage?

There really are no risks involved in trying Estrich's approach since there is no diet plan or even specific meal planning guidelines to use. Be prepared for a lot of comparisons to the law, court cases, and legal arguments. If that's not your cup of tea, then her arguments against being overweight and for dieting may leave you cold. On the other hand, they can

give you a new way to think about dieting, one that may provide the impetus you've needed. If you follow her general diet guidelines, however, you could easily fall short of calcium and vitamin

YES-YES'S
Determination, logic, and commitment

D, essential fatty acids, fiber, and some B vitamins. All of this is bad for your bones, your heart, and your bowels (constipation). You might be better off reading her book for motivation but following a diet plan that provides more of the nutrients you need.

Other Similar Diets

Because this is not really a diet plan but an inspirational book about women and weight loss, there is no other weight-loss diet quite like it.

The Metabolic Typing Diet

The Premise

This diet is based on the belief that there is no diet that will work for everyone. Rather, you must identify your metabolic type in order to choose the diet that will make you healthy and allow you to lose weight. The authors say that the USDA Food Guide Pyramid is mass-market nutrition, and they claim that our poor health, especially as we age, is a direct result of serious dietary deficiencies or imbalances that exist simply because we don't know what our individual nutrition needs are. Customized nutrition is the answer, they say, and they have devised a complicated system for identifying each person's metabolic type. Metabolic types are divided into three main categories according to the speed with which your body burns energy: slow oxidizers, fast oxidizers, and mixed oxidizers. According to the authors' theory, you can eat all of the best and highest quality organic foods, exercise regularly, drink plenty of fluids, get sufficient rest, and take the finest supplements money can buy, but you're

> ### Calorie Quota
> There are no calorie counts, only proportions of protein, fat, and carbohydrate for each diet type. If the overall guidelines are followed, however, any one of the three basic diet plans would likely result in cutting calories.

The Diet Is Best for: No one. The diet is not based on what we know about weight loss and metabolism, and it is complex and confusing to boot.

Who Should Not Try This Diet: Everyone should steer clear of this one. There's nothing here that will bring you better health or easy weight loss. The apparently arbitrary restrictions placed on certain fruits and vegetables are not healthy for seniors. Now that you're 50+, you need your diet to be as nutrient-dense as possible. Limiting the variety of nutrient-dense fruits and vegetables won't help you meet that goal.

still not going to feel well or enjoy optimum health unless you regularly obtain the nutrient balance that's right for you. By sticking to the correct metabolic diet plan, the authors promise relief from allergies, arthritis, headaches, low blood sugar, indigestion, cardiovascular problems, depression, and recurrent infections.

The Rationale

Their motto is, "One man's food is another man's poison." By identifying each person's metabolic type, the authors say you can address chronic health problems at their causative level, prevent illness, and rebuild long-lasting health. According to the plan, any given food or nutrient can have virtually opposite biochemical effects on different metabolic types. In keeping with that, lists of allowed and forbidden foods are provided for each metabolic type.

What's for Breakfast, Lunch, and Dinner?

What you're allowed to eat depends on your metabolic

type. Fast oxidizers are given a diet made up of 40 percent protein, 30 percent fat, and 30 percent carbohydrate. Slow oxidizers are prescribed a diet consisting of 25 percent protein, 15 percent fat, and 60 percent carbohydrate. Mixed oxidizers are given a diet with 30 percent of calories from protein, 20 percent from fat, and 50 percent from carbohydrate. But there's more to the diet than these three basic plans. You are supposed to "fine tune" the basic metabolic diets according to your circadian rhythm and blood type, as well as the glycemic index of the foods you eat and how you combine

---

Quick Take

- A complex diet system based on identifying your metabolic type

- Promises to alleviate health problems commonly associated with aging by regulating metabolism, stabilizing blood sugar, and balancing hormones

- Offers a detailed system of supplementation that depends on your metabolic type and current health status

---

foods in your diet. As a result, there actually are an infinite number of diet styles, and the book attempts to instruct dieters on how to accommodate them. Overall, the diet encourages the consumption of fruits, vegetables, and whole grains and discourages eating fatty foods and sugar. Five-day sample menus are provided for each of the three main metabolic types.

Fact or Fiction: What the Experts Say

This diet book has thrown in just about everything but the proverbial kitchen sink. While futurists predict a day in the not-too-distant future when we will be able to prescribe diets truly tailored to individual needs, taking into account genetics as well as lifestyle,

NO-NO'S

Forbidden foods vary depending on your metabolic classification.

calories are reduced and eating fruits and vegetables is encouraged. The disadvantage to these diet plans is their com-

YES-YES'S

Depends on your metabolic type. Fruits, vegetables, and whole grains are allowed and fluid and fiber intake encouraged.

that day has not yet arrived. All the talk about metabolic typing is premature, and the excruciatingly detailed plan laid out in this book is based on nothing more than conjecture. Overall, most of what's recommended in terms of actual food intake is not bad, but the diet for "fast oxidizers" is too high in protein and the carbohydrate diet is too low in fat for most people to stick with.

Gains and Losses/ What's the Damage?

Following any of the diet plans outlined in this book would likely result in weight loss, since many sources of excess fat and

plexity. With so many do's and don'ts, they are confusing, and it would be easy to find yourself falling short of certain nutrients. The mixed oxidizer diet appears to be the most balanced of the bunch. Dairy is generally discouraged, making it tough for most people to get enough calcium and vitamin D—two nutrients of particular importance to seniors—without supplements.

Other Similar Diets
Eat Right 4 Your Type

The 90/10 Weight-Loss Plan

The Premise

Registered dietitian Joy Bauer, the author of the 90/10 plan, says that years of developing nutrition plans for clients have convinced her that there is no diet that will magically melt fat away. The key to weight loss, she says, is to sensibly cut calories, and that's why she developed the 90/10 plan. The "90" in her title stands for "90 percent sensible choice" and the "10" for "10 percent fun food choices," which allows for some flexibility and indulgence. Bauer believes that no matter what the diet, you won't stick with it for long if you're not already used to eating that way. She asserts that carbohydrates will not make you fat—disputing the claims of low-carbohydrate diets—and that including them in your diet will, in fact, make weight loss easier while keeping your energy level up. While her diet

This Diet Is Best for: People who find it impossible to give up a little junk food treat every day but otherwise are willing to stick with a balanced, low-calorie plan

Who Should Not Try This Diet: Those who find it tough to stop once they've started eating cookies, chips, or cake. Total abstinence from forbidden foods might work best for them.

discourages eating refined carbohydrates such as sugar and candy, the 10 percent rule allows for what she calls "soul-soothing" foods that aren't exactly healthful. The diet is a realistic food strategy, not exact math. The program places more of an emphasis on exercise than most diet plans.

The Rationale

Bauer says the reason her plan works is because it's realistic. Any diet that forbids favorite foods is an invitation to "cheat," which is followed by guilt and surrender to old eating habits. By allowing 10 percent leeway in choosing some typically forbidden foods, it gives dieters freedom of choice. Exercise is also an integral part of the plan. There are factors such as heredity, age, frame, and metabolism, over which Bauer says you have no control. Her diet focuses on the factors that you can control, such as food intake, exercise, and your metabolism. While you can't control the inherited part of your basic metabolism, she says, you can increase your metabolic rate through exercise. Her suggestions for physical activity range from walking to weight training. The point, she says, is to exercise regularly. She provides lots of tips for warming up and even provides forms for keeping track of your activities.

What's for Breakfast, Lunch, and Dinner?

The 90/10 plan offers more menus than most other diets. It provides two weeks' worth

Calorie Quota

There are three different calorie levels to start out with: 1,200, 1,400, and 1,600 calories, based on the amount of weight you want to lose and how fast you want to lose it. Calorie counting is incorporated into the diet plan—assuming you stick with the menus.

of menus for each of the three calorie levels (1,200, 1,400, and 1,600). The lowest-calorie diet plan is for women who exercise little and who have only two to ten pounds to lose and want to lose it fast. The 1,400 calorie plan is for most women with moderately active lifestyles and who have between 2 and 50 pounds to lose. The 1,600 calorie plan works well for most men, whether they exercise or not, and women who are 5'6" or taller. A lengthy list of fun foods that can account for one serving (250 calories) a day is also provided. As long as you don't exceed the serving size specified, just about all of your favorite foods are allowed. The menus are pretty bland compared to a lot of other diet plans, and the amount of food is fairly small. On the 1,400 calorie plan, a typical day might include scrambled tofu and a toasted whole-wheat English muffin for breakfast; pita pizza for lunch; a baked apple for a snack; fish, sweet potato, and green beans for dinner; and a fun food at some point during the day.

Quick Take

- Low-calorie, mostly balanced diet

- Relatively low in fruits and vegetables

- Allows a once-a-day controlled splurge on junk food

- Limits refined carbohydrates, aside from the "Fun Food" daily splurge

---

Fact or Fiction: What the Experts Say

The diet is a relatively balanced, low-calorie plan. However, it falls far short of the recommend intakes for calcium and vitamin D, and it doesn't provide enough fruits, vegetables, and whole grains each day to meet current recommendations. Experts say that the calories "spent" on the daily allowance of "fun food" would be better spent on more

NO-NO'S

Eating more than the allowed "fun food" daily serving, going over the calorie count

fruits, vegetables, and whole grains. Add a little more produce each day, along with a calcium and vitamin D supplement, and the nutrition would be much improved. The 90/10 plan gets a gold star for its emphasis on physical activity and the flexibility it allows in designing your own activity plan.

Gains and Losses/ What's the Damage?

Bauer promises a weight loss of up to ten pounds during the first two weeks, depending on how much you have to lose and how low you go on calories.

After the initial rapid weight loss, you can expect to settle in to a loss of about one to two pounds per week. If you follow the diet for an

YES-YES'S

Following preset calorie limits, keeping a written record of what you eat, regular exercise, using a predetermined number of calories each day for a junk food splurge

extended period of time without taking a calcium and vitamin D supplement, you could be putting yourself at risk for osteoporosis. And the lack of high-fiber carbs at the lowest calorie level could cause constipation, an often troublesome problem for folks over 50.

Other Similar Diets

Weight Watchers

Nutri/System

The Premise

Nutri/System began 30 years ago as just another diet program offering prepackaged meals and dietary counseling. But three years ago, it morphed into an almost exclusively online weight-loss program (www.nutrisystem.com), complete with online counseling and menu planning. Membership in the online weight-loss community is free of charge. Newcomers are assigned a personal weight-loss counselor, who will track their progress and give advice as long as they follow the program. New members also receive a menu plan, a catalog of products, a food diary, a weight chart, an online weekly newsletter, and a few other goodies to get started. Other services include NutriBuddy groups, chat room support groups, and a virtual exercise instructor, which allows you to store your own customized exercise program. You can purchase prepackaged entrees and snacks, but unlike Jenny Craig, they are not mandatory. However, Nutri/System's menus incorporate its NuCuisine foods throughout, making it difficult to

Calorie Quota
Calorie levels are calculated individually but do not go below 1,000 calories a day. The average calorie intake, according to the company, is 1,200 for women and 1,500 for men.

follow the plan without buying the products.

The Rationale

Like Jenny Craig, the rationale is that preplanned menus incorporating prepackaged, preportioned foods make it easier to stick with a weight-loss program. Nutri/System's shift to an online dieting service offers more flexibility to people with irregular schedules and little free time to attend meetings. Dieters are never more than a few clicks away from information and support. Members can also talk to fellow Nutri/System dieters for support.

What's for Breakfast, Lunch, and Dinner?

Like Jenny Craig, the Nutri/System diet consists of 20 percent protein, 20 percent fat, and 60 percent carbohydrate. Each diet plan allows for three meals, two snacks, and one dessert each day. There are more than 100 different prepackaged, shelf-stable, microwavable NuCuisine entrees and snacks to choose from. You can make your own menus from the prepackaged foods or you can choose from six diet meal packages suited to different tastes. These packages provide all the basics from which to build your diet for

The Diet Is Best for: People whose schedules don't allow them to attend regular meetings and who want the flexibility of accessing support online almost any time

Who Should Not Try This Diet: People who need the one-on-one support that face-to-face counseling provides or the interaction of group meetings, and those on a strict budget

seven days. The meal plans are based on low fat food choices from the USDA Food Guide Pyramid. You add a specific number of servings of fruits, vegetables, and dairy products to them. The products are shelf-stable, a definite plus as long as you have access to a microwave oven. However, they won't taste as good as frozen or fresh foods.

Nutri/System offers a nutritional supplement to help fill the nutrient gaps, but it's a proprietary blend of nutrients and herbs. You'd be better off purchasing a conventional multivitamin.

Fact or Fiction: What the Experts Say

Most experts who express reservations about Nutri/System have the same concerns that they have about Jenny Craig—that all the preplanned menus with packaged foods may provide too much of a crutch for the dieter to ever go it alone. Few who start the diet expect to buy NuCuisine foods forever. But the program does offer some real advantages.

Janet Helm, M.S., R.D., a Chicago-based dietitian and spokesperson for the American Dietetic Association, says chat rooms and online counseling have been helpful in other areas, so these tools may prove to be useful in weight loss as well. And, as with any prepackaged diet plan, it offers the no-brainer

---

Quick Take

- Online weight-loss support program

- Includes lots of fruits, vegetables, and low fat dairy products

- Offers prepackaged, shelf-stable entrees and snacks; however, these are not required to follow the program

- Encourages physical activity and helps to set up an exercise plan based on your lifestyle and goals

approach as a kickstart to a long-term goal of weight loss.

Gains and Losses/ What's the Damage?

Anyone who follows the Nutri/System diet plan will get a well-balanced, reduced-

NO-NO'S

High fat, high-sugar foods; full-fat dairy products; inactivity

YES-YES'S

Lots of fruits and vegetables in addition to NuCuisine entrees and snacks

calorie diet that, combined with regular physical activity, should result in weight loss of one to two pounds per week. The diet was developed in accordance with weight-loss recommendations from the American Dietetic Association and the National Institutes of Health. One small study of the Nutri/System program found that postmenopausal women who followed a 1,200-calorie plan for 16 weeks lost an average of 21 pounds. The Nutri/System

NuCuisine foods cost about $55 a week, so you need to examine your budget before signing on to the program. And steer clear of the Herbal Pf products. They contain ephedra, which can have dangerous effects on blood pressure, increasing your risk for stroke and even causing death. The diet falls short on whole grains, which could make it low in fiber and contribute to constipation. And the 1,000- and 1,200-calorie diet plans, while balanced, are not enough to meet your over-50 nutrient needs.

Other Similar Diets

Jenny Craig, Weight Watchers

STICK-TO-IT-ABILITY RATING: 1 **2** 3 4 5

The Okinawa Program

The Premise

This is not a weight-loss program; it's a health-promoting program that, if followed, should result in weight loss. Cutting calories, however, is a major tenet of the program. It's based on the findings of a quarter century of research of the population of Okinawa, home of the longest-lived people in the world. According to the authors, the findings of the Okinawa Centenarian Study show that heart disease rates are minimal and the incidence of breast and prostate cancer is so rare that screening mammography is not needed and most aging men have never heard of prostate cancer. Okinawans also have the least amount of coronary heart disease, stroke, and cancer in the world. Researchers believe that Oki-

This Diet Is Best for: People who want to completely overhaul their diet and lifestyle, including finding a renewed sense of spirituality and community. The program calls for a total commitment of body and soul to improve health and increase longevity.

Who Should Not Try This Diet: Those who are only interested in making minor adjustments in eating habits or are not willing to try new foods

nawans' extraordinarily long and healthy lives are the result of the "healthiest diet in the world" as well as their psychospiritual focus and an integrative system of health care that uses the best of Western and Eastern medical practices. While genes are responsible for up to one-third of the diseases of premature aging, they say that diet and lifestyle—factors we can control—are responsible for the other two-thirds.

Calorie Quota

There are no calorie counts, just dietary guidelines based on the authors' Okinawa Food Pyramid, along with recommended menus, food lists, portion sizes, and recipes. The authors recommend eating only until you are 80 percent full.

The Rationale

A greater percentage of Okinawans live to the age of 100 and beyond than any other people in the world, and the authors believe that if we follow their example, we can do the same. That means we should adopt not just their diet but their lifestyle, too. Okinawans eat a low fat, low calorie, high fiber diet, and they place a priority on exercise, family relationships, and spiritual connectedness. Studies show that when Okinawans adopt a more Western diet and lifestyle, their rates of overweight and illness increase and their life expectancy decreases. As a result, the authors devote a significant part of the book to spirituality. The authors believe that stress, anxiety, and a feeling of helplessness contribute to poor health and cut our lives short.

What's for Breakfast, Lunch, and Dinner?

The authors have devised a food pyramid based on the diet of the Okinawan people.

Rather than classifying foods simply as fruits, vegetables, and grains, as other food pyramids do, the Okinawa pyramid breaks the groupings down further into foods rich in flavonoids, calcium, or omega-3 fatty acids. Its base consists of grains—mainly whole grains—and vegetables, and it includes a lot of foods that are rich in flavonoids (phytonutrients). Overall, the diet provides 50 percent or more of calories from complex carbohydrates and encourages consumption of plant foods over animal foods. Though the diet is high in carbohydrates, it recommends avoiding carbohydrate foods with a high glycemic index (those that raise blood sugar the most) because they contribute to heart disease and obesity. A generous four weeks' worth of menus are provided, and allowances are made for those not quite ready to make the leap to a Far East way of eating. The book also provides about 80 low fat, low-calorie recipes.

> ## Quick Take
>
> - A total diet and lifestyle program based on Eastern philosophies and dietary habits
> - A mostly plant-based diet that's rich in complex carbohdyrates and high in fiber
> - Considers stress reduction and building a support system essential to good health and longevity

Fact or Fiction: What the Experts Say

Most of the advice in the Okinawan Program is consistent with what the majority of experts advise we do to live longer, healthier lives. But it's doubtful that the majority of people who want to lose weight are ready to make such dramatic changes in their diets, lifestyles, and even their basic approach to life. To make effective changes, say experts, a diet program must first and foremost be realistic.

NO-NO'S

Overly processed, refined foods; a lot of meat and eggs; trans fatty acids found in processed foods

Gains and Losses/What's the Damage?

Like most diets based on eliminating sugar and excess fat and eating minimally processed high-fiber plant foods, the Okinawa Program will result in weight loss if it's consistently followed. The diet is well-balanced, but the authors wisely suggest a multi-vitamin for nutritional insurance. The diet is lower in calcium than most experts recommend, but that's because the authors subscribe to the theory that a diet low in animal protein and sodium coupled with a physically active lifestyle requires less calcium than the recommended dietary allowance (RDA). Still, a calcium supplement would be a healthful addition,

YES-YES'S

Whole grains, vegetables, fruits, low glycemic-index foods, foods rich in omega-3 fatty acids, foods rich in flavonoid phytonutrients, tofu and other soy foods

especially if you're at risk for osteoporosis or don't intend to follow the program to the letter. One chapter is devoted to being lean and fit, with the focus on martial arts for their spiritual component and stress-reduction benefits.

Other Similar Diets

Eat More, Live Longer; Eat More, Weigh Less

STICK-TO-IT-ABILITY RATING: 1 2 **3** 4 5

The Origin Diet

The Premise

The Origin Diet: How Eating Like Our Stone Age Ancestors Will Maximize Your Health is based on the idea that we can live longer and healthier lives by more closely approximating the diet and activity level of our Stone Age ancestors. The author, dietitian Elizabeth Somer, says that eating too much food and not exercising enough are responsible for 70 percent of all cancers and at least 50 percent of heart disease. Middle-age spread, she assures us, is not related to age but to a lack of activity. Moreover, she believes it's possible to stave off the frailties of old age by following the Origin Diet. Specifically, Somer's diet promises to help prevent heart disease, cancer, high blood pressure, osteoporosis, cataracts, memory loss, and depression while boosting your energy and helping you to lose weight and live longer. Weight loss is not the focus of the Origin Diet, but it is a side benefit and integral to the life-extending premise of the plan.

Calorie Quota

The calorie content of food is not emphasized in the Origin Diet. Rather, learning how to choose a wide variety of high-fiber, nutrient-packed foods is the point. Eating more of these foods should make you eat less and ultimately cut calories.

The Rationale

There is a valid scientific basis for most of Somer's claims about the Origin Diet. Her diet encourages the consumption of whole, unprocessed foods, which research shows are rich in compounds called phytonutrients that are believed to help fight disease, and foods that are high in fiber, which can help control blood sugar and lower cholesterol. There's more to her plan than dietary recommendations, however. Somer offers "Five Stone Age Secrets" that will allow us to approximate the healthy lifestyle of our ancestors, one that she says is more genetically appropriate for us. *The Origin Diet* details how to alter your diet and lifestyle in order to adhere to these five principles. Physical activity is an integral part of the plan.

What's for Breakfast, Lunch, and Dinner?

Though the diet emphasizes what Somer calls "wild," or natural, foods you'll still find healthful canned, frozen, and even some highly processed foods such as fat-free bottled salad dressing on the menus. She offers several sample breakfast, lunch, and dinner menus that can be mixed and matched at the appropriate meals over several days, as well as recipes. There are no strict food exchanges or diet plans to

---

This Diet Is Best for: Anyone who is ready and willing to make some major changes in their diet and lifestyle. This diet is one that could benefit all.

Who Should Not Try This Diet: There's no one that the diet is unsafe for, but it can be expensive, so make sure you're willing and able to absorb the additional cost of the food required to stick to the plan. If you can't live without the occasional splurge, then this may not be the diet plan for you.

follow, but she does give some dietary guidelines. These include eating slowly and regularly and each day having six servings of whole grains, two to three servings of calcium-rich foods, three servings of starchy vegetables, and two servings of protein sources that are low in saturated fat. A typical breakfast might include soy milk, wheat germ, raisins, and chopped walnuts. Lunch might be a chicken breast sandwich on whole-wheat bread, a green salad with fat-free dressing, and nonfat milk. Dinner could include poached salmon with vegetables, a baked potato, broccoli, and nonfat milk. To cut back on unhealthy fats, she recommends eating only skinless poultry breast, fish, shellfish, and wild game as your meat sources. Somer also advocates grazing—eating five to six mini-meals throughout the day—rather than eating three large ones.

Fact or Fiction: What the Experts Say

Though no experts contend that the Origin Diet is unhealthy, some believe that asking people to stick almost completely to unprocessed food and to increase their intake of wild game as a protein source is carrying it a bit too far. However, if it's a plan you think you can stick with (and afford—game meat can be quite expensive) then it can't do anything but benefit your health and longevity. Somer's emphasis on physical activity and stress reduction gets her high marks from experts. She

---

Quick Take

- Based on what are believed to be the dietary habits of our Stone Age ancestors

- Focuses on unprocessed, whole-grain foods

- Recommends lots of physical activity

offers specific suggestions on how to incorporate regular activity into your daily life and ways to relax and relieve stress.

need for vitamin D increases with age, and again, fortified dairy products are your best source. If you switch to soy milk from cow's milk, be sure it's fortified with calcium and

NO-NO'S

Processed, refined foods; saturated fats in meats and whole-fat dairy products; fast food; inactivity

YES-YES'S

Whole grains, fresh fruits and vegetables, legumes, wild game meats, olive oil, canola oil

Gains and Losses/What's the Damage?

The diet is generally quite healthy, including lots of fruits, vegetables, whole grains, and soy foods. The only nutrients in which the diet might be deficient are calcium and vitamin D. While the basic guidelines of the diet recommend two to three servings of dairy a day, more than many diet plans, that's not enough to meet the recommended intake of 1,200 to 1,500 milligrams for people 50 and older. The same is true of vitamin D. Your

vitamin D; not all soy milks are. Though this diet doesn't call for calorie counting or food exchanges, chances are you won't eat too much. The foods included in the diet are mostly unprocessed and high in fiber, so you'll likely feel full faster and be less likely to overeat. Physical activity is as much a part of the Origin Diet as the diet itself.

Other Similar Diets

Eat More, Weight Less; Turn Off the Fat Genes

Overeaters Anonymous

The Premise

Overeaters Anonymous describes itself as a "fellowship of individuals who, through shared experience, strength, and hope, are recovering from compulsive overeating." It is an international, nonprofit organization that operates through a network of volunteers. Its main function is to offer a support system for people trying to overcome compulsive overeating and to spread the message of hope and recovery to those who are suffering in silence. The organization has no diet plan or diet book, and as a result, there is no calorie counting or recipe exchanging, no sharing of diet-ing tips, and no membership dues or fees. There currently are about 7,000 groups meeting in more than 52 countries around the world. Overeaters Anonymous (OA) is completely self-supported through contributions and the sale of publications, one of which is an international monthly magazine called *Lifeline*, which includes true stories by OA members.

The Rationale

Compulsive overeating is viewed by OA as an addiction, like drinking or gambling, and is treated as such.

Thi Diet Is Best for: There is no diet, but a survey of the program's membership found that OA members are typically middle-aged women who have been struggling with compulsive overeating since their teens. The program is designed for people who have serious problems controlling their food intake and need the support of people in the same situation. You can determine if you are a compulsive eater who might be helped by the 12-step program by taking OA's questionnaire.

Who Should Not Try This Diet: Overeaters Anonymous is not for someone just trying to lose a few pounds or even for someone who needs to lose quite a bit of weight that was gained through a gradual increase in calorie intake or a drop in activity or both. This is for people who admit to having serious problems with food and likely have the emotional baggage that comes with that. OA is not for those who may be uncomfortable or disagree with the spiritual and religious aspects of the program.

In fact, the OA program is modeled after the 12-step program for Alcoholics Anonymous, which addresses physical, emotional, and spiritual recovery. The only requirement for becoming a member of OA is a desire to

stop eating compulsively. As with Alcoholics Anonymous, each member has a sponsor, someone who is already a recovering member of OA. There is a strong spiritual component to the group, and members must be willing to "surrender" themselves to God (not a particular god, but their personal concept of a higher power), as the ultimate authority over their destiny.

What's for Breakfast, Lunch, and Dinner?

There is no diet plan or calorie counting. In fact, no diet recommendations are made at all, except for the encouragement to stop compulsive overeating and to develop a personal eating plan based on your own likes, dislikes, and lifestyle. In fact, the organization says that

Quick Take

- Designed for people with a history of uncontrollable food intake and obesity

- No specific diet plan, though the organization recommends that each member develops one with the assistance of a nutritionist

- Requires members to follow a 12-step program modeled after Alcoholics Anonymous

"individual plans of eating are as varied as our members." Though every chapter is different, the organization recommends that all members consult a qualified professional for help in creating an individual diet plan.

Fact or Fiction: What the Experts Say

Some experts have reservations about the loosely knit organi-

Calorie Quota

Because there is no diet plan, there are no daily calorie counts or menu plans.

YES-YES'S	NO-NO'S
Attending meetings, stopping compulsive overeating while following the 12-step program, staying in contact with your sponsor	Continuing to compulsively overeat and failing to attend meetings

if attending OA meetings will result in weight loss. However, for people who have serious issues with food and a history of compulsive overeating, the group meetings may offer additional support during recovery.

zation and the rule-free atmosphere OA offers. And some argue that while it may make a person feel less guilty about their compulsive eating, it does nothing to address and "fix" the underlying problems. Others, however, say that if it offers much needed support, that alone may make membership in OA worthwhile.

Gains and Losses/What's the Damage?

Because there is no diet plan, there's no way to assess

Other Similar Diets

Since OA is not really a diet plan, there are no other similar programs. However, it is modeled after the 12-step programs of Alcoholics Anonymous and Gamblers Anonymous.

The RealAge Diet

The Premise

Dr. Michael Roizen's second youth-enhancing diet book, *RealAge: Make Yourself Younger With What You Eat*, promises that you can make yourself biologically younger than your chronological age by eating the right foods. He says this isn't a diet book; in fact, he calls it a "non-diet diet." Instead, it promotes healthy eating, which allows you to lose weight. Together, these two aspects will add not just years but healthy years to your life.

The Rationale

The idea is that if you eat the right foods, you can stave off or delay chronic debilitating diseases, such as heart disease, diabetes, and cancer, and look and feel younger, longer.

This Diet Is Best for: Those who are very motivated and willing to make some serious changes to improve their health. It's packed with good information about food and nutrition.

Who Should Not Try This Diet: Those whose main motivation is weight loss. It's designed for people who are ready and willing to make permanent changes in their diet and lifestyle in order to extend their healthy years. Weight loss is simply a part of the equation.

Roizen sums up his eating philosophy early on when he says, "Eat nutrient rich, calorie poor, and delicious." To calculate your "real age" (your biological age not your chronological age), Roizen provides a 20+ page quiz that demonstrates just how many factors comprise a healthful diet as well as the interrelationship between them. Taking a single supplement or focusing on a single food or food group won't help you lose weight, nor will it help delay aging. Roizen also advocates eating meals in a stress-free and enjoyable environment.

What's for Breakfast, Lunch, and Dinner?

There are no gimmicks to the RealAge diet—just principles for healthful eating. Some of the diet basics that Roizen says will add years to your life include avoiding red meat, saturated fats, trans fats, simple sugars, and empty calories.

Overall, RealAge dieters are encouraged to avoid foods with a high glycemic index (foods that cause a sudden surge in insulin levels). Some believe high glycemic-index foods cause weight gain.

Roizen provides about 20 recipes and 2 weeks' worth of sample menus. A typical day may include kashi, blueberries, soy milk, and orange juice for breakfast; soy nut butter and whole-fruit spread on whole-wheat bread, a plum, and soy milk for lunch; a salad with avocado, canned tuna, and nuts with olive oil

> ### Calorie Quota
> Roizen doesn't emphasize counting calories, but he does provide calorie counts and serving sizes for a few basic foods. He also provides a standard chart of calorie needs by height, activity level, and weight along with a chart showing the number of calories burned during various physical activities.

dressing, whole-grain crackers, and a glass of red wine for dinner; strawberries dipped in a little dark chocolate for dessert; and a whole-wheat pretzel with mustard for a snack. While the recipes and menus provide a basis for altering your diet, there is no system for creating your own RealAge diet. That is up to you. Altogether, Roizen points out 127 factors that affect the rate of aging; 25 of them have to do with exercise and diet, and he outlines what to do and what to avoid to work these factors to your favor.

Fact or Fiction: What the Experts Say

Roizen's diet is a healthful one that promises to boost your

> ## Quick Take
>
> - Designed to promote good health and longevity through diet
>
> - Increases your intake of fruits, vegetables, whole grains, legumes, and soy foods while still allowing for the occasional treat and a glass of wine with dinner
>
> - Emphasizes enjoying healthy food in a relaxed atmosphere

intake of phytochemicals, natural disease-preventing compounds found in plant foods. Research clearly shows that such a diet should reduce your risk of developing several chronic and sometimes deadly diseases. It's doubtful, however, that Roizen has perfected the formula for calculating exactly how many extra years you can expect to live by changing your diet, as he implies with his detailed questionnaire and complex scoring system. He says, for example, that eating foods rich in flavonoids (a phytochemical), such as apples, onions, broccoli, garlic, chocolate, or grapes, will make your RealAge exactly 3.2 years younger. Roizen says that every recommendation made in the book is backed up by scientific evidence. However, there's no research that backs up his very specific calculations of how many years you will add or take away from your life, depending on how you eat or live your life. However, the questionnaire does drive home the point that you may extend your life and your healthy years by making some serious changes in how and what you eat.

Gains and Losses/ What's the Damage?

There's little to fault with Roizen's diet. It's chock-full of fruits, vegetables, nuts, and whole grains. While the diet is quite nutritious, it responsibly recommends taking a multivitamin/min-eral supplement that does not contain excessive amounts of any one nutrient as a sort of nutritional insurance policy. Also to his credit, Roizen devotes an entire chapter to exercise and your activity level—and how often you exercise also figures into the RealAge for-mula. The book devotes quite a bit of attention to two nutrients that are especially important as you age—vitamin D and calcium. He even goes so far as to say that vitamin D may be one of the most impor-tant vitamins in your age-reduction plan.

NO-NO'S
High glycemic-index foods, foods high in trans fats

YES-YES'S
Low glycemic-index foods, fruits and vegeta-bles, relaxed atmosphere while eating, a balanced multivitamin

Other Similar Diets
The Origin Diet; Eat, Drink, and Be Healthy

Richard Simmons

The Premise

Richard Simmons is hard to miss, so chances are you've heard about or seen him even if you weren't thinking about losing weight. He's been the star of several television shows, infomercials, and videos, and he has written an autobiography. For some, his explosive enthusiasm is hard to take. His diet is a healthful one for the 50+ crowd, but there is little that's unique about Richard Simmons' diet plan other than Simmons himself. His diet plan is updated regularly and repackaged; the latest version is called *Richard Simmons' Lose Weight and Celebrate*. The program, which is available from TV infomercials currently on QVC and his Web site (www.richardsimmons.com), includes three exercise videos

with Broadway musical themes, a small cookbook, a dietary instruction booklet, a sample introductory pack of Simmons' energy-boosting supplements, and the *FoodMover Gold*, a useful little handheld plastic device that allows you to keep track of your daily food allowances, water intake, and exercise expenditures. The exercise videos are unique in that they feature people of all ages, sizes, and shapes. Having been extremely over-weight himself, Simmons obviously empathizes with anyone who's unhappy about their weight.

The Rationale

With Richard Simmons as your personal cheerleader, you

may find the motivation you need to get with the program and to stick with it. His overriding philosophy is one of inclusiveness. No matter how overweight you are or how miserable you feel because of your weight, Simmons reassuringly offers hope. Register as a member on his Web site (it's $9.95 a month), and you can join dieters' chat rooms and an occasional live chat with Simmons himself. There are lots of extras, including grocery lists, an online *FoodMover*, and many more recipes than those provided in the original kit. You can also order the *Lose Weight and Celebrate* program online. Simmons places a tremendous emphasis on physical activity, and this is the one trait of his weight-loss program that stands out and puts it a notch above the rest. In fact, Richard Simmons was, and probably still is, best known for his exercise videos. If you're over 50 and out of shape, check with your doctor

Calorie Quota

The minimum number of calories is 1,200, but caloric intake can be adjusted much higher by adding more food allowances.

This Diet Is Best for: People who find Richard Simmons appealing and inspiring and those who prefer no-nonsense, no-frills diet plans

Who Should Not Try This Diet: Anyone who finds Richard Simmons hard to take and anyone who feels group meetings or individual counseling sessions are essential before you start his exercise program. Some of the exercise routines really get your heart going.

What's for Breakfast, Lunch, and Dinner?

The *Lose Weight and Celebrate* program lays out a well-balanced and varied diet that admirably includes a minimum of seven servings of fruits and vegetables and two servings of low fat dairy foods a day. He also wisely recommends drinking eight glasses of water each day and not going below 1,200 calories. It's a no-nonsense program that sets clear guidelines but leaves individual food choices up to the dieter. There are no prepackaged foods, and he encourages you to choose from fresh foods like fish, strawberries, greens, oranges, and whole-grain breads. The foods are grouped according to categories, and the diet is set up much like the exchange system used by diabetics. You're allowed a certain number of food exchanges from each group, depending on your daily calorie quota.

Fact or Fiction: What the Experts Say

Bonnie Taub-Dix, R.D., a nutrition consultant in private practice in New York City, says she believes the Richard Simmons program makes sense and is not extreme. Plus, she gives him

Quick Take

- Personality-driven diet that provides the energy and motivation to keep dieters going

- A philosophy of inclusion, offering hope to even the most overweight and sedentary who want to succeed at weight loss

- A well-balanced diet that offers both flexibility and variety

- Places a major emphasis on physical activity

extra points because he acknowledges and accommodates the needs of even the most overweight people. Few experts take real issue with any of Richard Simmons' programs, with the exception of the inclusion and marketing of his own brand of supplements.

NO-NO'S
Low self-esteem or being critical of yourself, eating less than the recommended amounts of food, inactivity

YES-YES'S
8 glasses of water a day, 7 servings of fruits and vegetables, 2 servings of low fat dairy, regular exercise

Gains and Losses/ What's the Damage?

Those who follow Simmons' diet could run a little low on calcium and vitamin D, even though it includes more dairy than many other weight-loss programs. If you follow his diet plan, be sure to include a calcium and vitamin D supplement to help fend off osteoporosis and compensate for your body's reduced ability to produce active vitamin D. As admirable as the program is overall, Simmons loses face

over the addition of his own brand of supposedly energy-boosting supplements, which are hawked by a telemarketer soon after you place your order for the program. Ignore the hype and go for a regular over-the-counter multivitamin. Simmons' plan is good for any age. If you follow his recommended calorie intakes, you should expect to lose about one to two pounds per week.

Other Similar Diets
Weight Watchers

STICK-TO-IT-ABILITY RATING: **1 2** 3 4 5

The Schwarzbein Principle

The Premise

As suggested by the subtitle, *The Truth About Weight Loss, Health and Aging*, this book is about adjusting your diet to curb disease, turn back the biological clock, and lose weight. Endocrinologist Diana Schwarzbein offers her own version of a high-protein, low-carbohydrate diet that she says will help control insulin. High insulin levels, the result of a high-carbohydrate, low fat diet, are responsible for a wide variety of ills, accelerate the aging process, turn off your metabolism, and cause weight gain, food cravings, depression, and mood swings, according to Schwarzbein. Instead of using a food pyramid model, she has developed a food box representing four food groups—proteins, fats, nonstarchy vegetables, and carbohydrates—which need to be eaten together in the proper amounts to balance the body's hormone systems. Sugar, says Schwarzbein, is addictive. To complement her diet plan, she recommends a variety of sup-

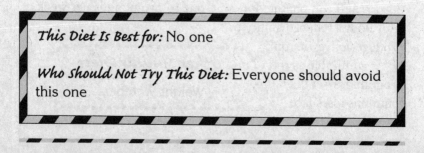

This Diet Is Best for: No one

Who Should Not Try This Diet: Everyone should avoid this one

plements, including a multivitamin, magnesium, calcium, 5-hydroxytryptophan, and essential fatty acids.

The Rationale

The basic principle behind Schwarzbein's "healing" diet plan is using a diet that's high in protein and healthy fats and low in carbohydrates to control insulin and glucagon levels.

Glucagon is a hormone that causes blood sugar to rise, and insulin is a hormone that brings blood sugar levels back down. She says that you can balance and control hormones in the body that affect food cravings and metabolism by eating right. You can lower insulin levels by exercising and eating "good" oils and fats and fiber. Levels of serotonin (a chemical produced by the body that regulates nerve impulses in the brain) can be regulated by avoiding alcohol, caffeine, refined carbohydrates, chocolate, and sugar. The result, she says, is reduced cravings. Carbohydrate calories are limited because she believes that it's impossible to overeat protein and "good" fats. Only carbohydrates cause insulin levels to rise too much, which triggers weight gain. Sugar is blamed for interfering with the body's use of nutrients and keeping insulin levels high.

Calorie Quota

No calorie counts are provided and limited information is given about serving sizes, making it difficult to estimate what your actual calorie intake would be.

What's for Breakfast, Lunch, and Dinner?

The diet provides four weeks' worth of sample menus for the "healing program," which Schwarzbein says reverses insulin resistance and repairs your metabolism. She also provides four weeks' worth of menus and recipes for vegetarians. The menus are designed to keep your insulin-to-glucagon ratio and your glycemic index balanced by providing only 15 grams of carbohydrates per meal and by including foods from the four designated food groups in the proper proportions. A typical day's menu might include scrambled eggs and sausage, oatmeal with butter and cream, and sliced tomatoes for breakfast; cobb salad with olive oil and vinegar dressing and an apple for lunch; and roast pork loin, brown rice with butter, asparagus with butter, and a mixed-greens salad with olive oil and vinegar dressing for dinner. Two snacks are allowed, one of sunflower seeds and another of almonds and string cheese.

Quick Take

- A high-protein, high fat diet

- Prohibits refined carbohydrates and other high glycemic-index foods

- Claims to regulate hormone levels in the body

- Recommends choosing foods that you could, in theory, pick, gather, milk, or hunt or fish for

Fact or Fiction: What the Experts Say

The Schwarzbein Principle is basically a variation on several other high-protein, low-carb diets. If weight loss results it's due to a reduced calorie intake, not a dietary manipulation of hormones. Carbohydrate intake is so restricted that it could be energy draining. And the levels of cholesterol and saturated fat in the diet far exceed what almost all experts recommend for a heart-healthy diet. There is no proof, say experts, that following this diet will exert some sort of hormonal control over your body that will speed weight loss and ultimately slow the aging process.

Gains and Losses/ What's the Damage?

Whether or not weight loss would actually result is unclear from the menu plans, since portion sizes, it would be easy to actually gain weight on this diet. Don't expect to lose weight fast, even if you're keeping your total calorie intake in check. Because of the limitations placed on

NO-NO'S

Refined man-made carbohydrates, foods with a high glycemic index (foods that raise blood sugar levels the most), most vegetable oils, processed or high-sodium sausages, processed foods that contain hydrogenated fats

YES-YES'S

High-protein, high fat foods; limited amounts of whole grains and starchy vegetables; hormone-free, antibiotic-free, range-fed meat and poultry

recommended serving sizes for many foods, including high-calorie foods, are not provided. Despite what Schwarzbein says about not focusing on calorie counts, if you eat too many calories, you'll gain weight. With the menus provided and the limited information on several nutrient-rich foods, the diet could easily fall short of several nutrients, including calcium, vitamin D, folic acid, and fiber.

Other Similar Diets

Dr. Atkins' Age-Defying Diet, The Age-Free Zone

Dr. Shapiro's Picture Perfect Weight Loss

The Premise

Dr. Howard M. Shapiro, a weight-loss doctor to the rich and famous in New York City, has developed a weight-loss strategy that helps dieters develop "food awareness." By visually demonstrating the choices you can make in your diet (one fat-free, sugar-free muffin has the same number of calories as 1 whole pineapple, ½ cantaloupe, 2 pears, ½ papaya, 5 ounces grapes, ½ kiwifruit, and 2 whole-wheat rolls together, for instance), Shapiro says you'll be able to make better food choices—choices that will allow you to eat any food you want and yet lose weight. In more than 100 pages of photographs, he shows you how to get more food for fewer calories. In his 20 years of counseling people about losing weight, Shapiro says he has learned that there is no single weight-loss program that can work for everyone.

> ### Calorie Quota
> There is no set calorie count. There are a few "before" and "after" menus that show dieters saving as much as 2,500 calories a day by following suggested substitutions.

The Rationale

The rationale behind Shapiro's diet is one found in several other diet plans—it's the calorie concentration of foods that is the key to controlling weight. You can eat more of foods that have a lower calorie concentration than you can of those with a higher calorie concentration. Through clear explanations and graphic illustrations, Shapiro shows you which kinds of foods are more concentrated. And he dispels a lot of myths about low-calorie choices. Think you're being virtuous by having a dry bagel? Well, it turns out that only one-third of that dry bagel provides the same number of calories as a vegetarian ham sandwich on light bread with lettuce, tomato, mustard, and a pickle. The sandwich will fill you up more, and it also is more nutritious. Shapiro frowns upon deprivation because it leads to cravings, which lead to overeating. Instead he recommends that you understand the choices you make and adjust your diet accordingly. He considers portion cutting an "ill-advised exercise in a false kind of willpower." You don't need to have smaller portions but rather larger portions of

This Diet Is Best for: People with a lot of self-control and determination. Even if you decide not to follow his plan, the visuals can help you make lower-calorie substitutions.

Who Should Not Try This Diet: If you're looking for specific day-to-day guidance on what to eat and what not to eat, then this diet may not be for you. However, if you can take this book as a starting-off point and you're willing to do a little calorie and serving size research of your own, you may find it helpful. If not, you could end up getting far more calories than you should.

lower-calorie food. He doesn't discourage eating carbohydrates—either sugar or starch, asserting that a calorie is a calorie, no matter what it is made of or when you eat it. Shapiro encourages dieters to keep a food diary to increase their food awareness.

What's for Breakfast, Lunch, and Dinner?

The diet allows anything your heart desires, as long as you keep your calorie count under control. While it gives no guidelines for daily calorie intakes, it encourages dieters to stick with low-calorie foods that are high in volume. He doesn't offer any menu plans, recipes, or food exchanges. According to Shapiro, there are no bad foods and there are no correct portions. It's all up to your ability to visualize the calorie counts and portion sizes of foods and make the right choices.

Fact or Fiction: What the Experts Say

If you can trust the calorie comparisons in the photographs, then his idea makes some sense. Eating more for less (fewer calories) is a concept all nutritionists try to teach. But, according to Kathleen Zelman, R.D., nutrition consultant in Atlanta, Georgia, and a spokesperson for the American Dietetic Association, dieters should double-check the portions, since some of the photographs appear to underestimate the serving size of high-calorie foods and overes-

---

Quick Take

- Raises your awareness of food so you can make better choices

- Uses photographs to help you visualize your options

- Says there are no "bad" foods

- Has no calorie counting

timate the serving size of low-calorie foods. In addition, Shapiro's complete focus on

NO-NO'S

Everything is allowed, but the idea is to choose primarily those foods that are least calorically dense

over 50. Neither does he mention the possibility of getting too much of some nutrients, such as sodium. If you follow his concept carefully, you should lose weight and feel more satisfied, but

YES-YES'S

Eating for pleasure and satisfaction by choosing less calorie-dense foods

caloric density seems to overlook the nutrient density of foods. Choosing foods that offer the most nutrients for the fewest calories is also an important weight-loss strategy.

Gains and Losses/ What's the Damage?

Although Shapiro's basic idea is a good one, he seems to have sidestepped nutrition. Almost no consideration is given to making sure you get enough calcium, vitamin D, vitamin B_{12}, folic acid, or any of the other nutrients that are so important for your continued good health now that you're

there's no guarantee that you'll be getting all the nutrients you need. One chapter of the book is devoted to exercise and gives a broad overview of how to get fit. While it's more information than some diets offer, there is very little in terms of day-to-day guidelines on what kind of exercise to do and how much of it to do.

Other Similar Diets

Volumetrics,
The Pritikin Principle

Slim•Fast

The Premise

Though there are lots of liquid diets around—some of which are medically supervised and some, like Slim•Fast, which are not—they all basically offer quick weight loss by substituting a sweet-tasting nutritionally fortified shake or bar for a meal. In the past, liquid diets developed a bad reputation because dieters were restricting their intake to only 500 to 800 calories a day and getting sick—even dying— as a result of their weight-loss efforts. But the liquid diet industry has cleaned up its act, and now companies like Slim•Fast, which has been around for more than 20 years, offer a safer program. Like many other diet programs, today Slim•Fast offers an online dieting community complete with an online weight-charting tool, coupons, a personal food and exercise diary, chat sessions with registered dietitians,

This Diet Is Best for: People who like the taste of Slim•Fast products and find the convenience of a portable meal-replacement shake or bar appealing

Who Should Not Try This Diet: Anyone who doesn't like fruit or milk shakes or needs to eat more volume at meals to feel satisfied. It's not for people who need counseling or other dieters to talk to, since it provides no face-to-face encounters for support.

a weekly newsletter, and the opportunity to hook up with an online Slim•Fast Buddy. There is no one-on-one counseling, however, either on- or offline. The Slim•Fast online community boasts almost 400,000 members.

The Rationale

Most liquid diets imply, if not promise, quick weight loss, suggesting you can satisfy your sweet tooth and curb your appetite at the same time with liquid meal replacements. Slim•Fast falls into that category, though as liquid diets go, it's one of the more responsible plans. Total calories don't go below 1,200 a day, and the plan includes lots of fruits and vegetables in addition to the Slim•Fast foods and snacks. Liquid diets are appealing because of their simplicity and convenience. For some people, that simplicity and convenience spell success.

What's for Breakfast, Lunch, and Dinner?

Slim•Fast's meal replacements make up two meals a day during the weight-loss phase of the plan. Buying the company's products, which include Ready-to-Drink shakes, Snack Bars, Meal-On-The-Go Bars, Slim•Fast Powders, Breakfast and Lunch Bars, and Juice-Based Ready-To-Drink Shakes (they contain only four percent real juice), then, is mandatory. You can find the products for sale online as well as in most supermarkets and drugstores. The 11-ounce shakes are the main attraction and cost about $1.25 each. The meal replacement bars cost about $1.00 each. Though dairy products are not part of the basic diet plan, the meal replacements are fortified with calcium, vitamin D, and riboflavin, as well as fiber. The products are low in fat (only about one to three grams per shake), but they also are high in sugar.

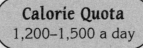

Calorie Quota
1,200–1,500 a day

Quick Take

- A liquid diet plan that centers around meal replacements and snacks

- Incorporates three servings of fruits and at least four servings of vegetables into the daily diet plan

- Offers two calorie levels: 1,200 and 1,500 calories a day

The one "real meal" a day allowed during the weight-loss phase consists of 4 to 6 ounces of poultry, fish, or lean meat; ½ baked potato; 1½ cups steamed vegetables; a large salad; and a piece of fruit. In addition to a Slim•Fast snack, two pieces of fruit are allowed as snacks each day.

As the dieter reaches goal weight, the plan allows regular foods at two meals a day, with a Slim•Fast meal replacement at only one meal a day. How-ever, there is no instruction for weaning yourself away from Slim•Fast products altogether, leaving dieters dependent on the products forever.

Fact or Fiction: What the Experts Say

The Slim•Fast diet should result in weight loss. But dieticians question whether any liquid diet can actually train people to eat right, which is what changing your eating habits should be all about, says Keith Ayoob, Ed.D, R.D., director of nutrition at the Rose F. Kennedy Center at Albert Einstein College of Medicine in New York City. Losing weight is simply a benefit of eating right, he says.

Gains and Losses/ What's the Damage?

If you follow the plan as suggested, a 1,200- to 1,500-calorie diet should result in a gradual weight loss for most people. However, for anyone who is extremely overweight, 1,200 to 1,500 calories may be

NO-NO'S

Regular foods at two meals a day; sweets, other than Slim•Fast shakes and bars

YES-YES'S

Slim•Fast products, fruits, and vegetables

too low to begin with and no formula is given for increasing the calorie level. Slim•Fast's informational brochures do mention physical activity, but they don't emphasize it enough. Slim•Fast's diet may be a useful starting point for some people who need a gimmick to get them going, but it offers very little education or advice about entering the real world of fast food, restaurants, and family get-togethers, nor does it offer tips for permanently adjusting eating habits.

Because the diet is centered around Slim•Fast products, with only one "real meal" a day, your diet could fall short of fiber (even though Slim•Fast products have some fiber added) and lead to constipation. Though the products are also fortified with a variety of vitamins and minerals, they don't contain all the disease-preventing phytonutrients found naturally in food. Most of the products are also quite high in sugar—not good if you've already got high blood sugar or insulin resistance. In addition, the Slim•Fast products are fortified with iron, a nutrient you don't need more of now that you're 50 or older. And if you opt for the 1,200-calorie-a-day plan, it's unlikely to provide all the nutrients your body needs without a multivitamin supplement.

Other Similar Diets

Cambridge Diet

SugarBusters!

The Premise

This diet book has become a virtual classic among calorie counters, especially those who believe that sugar is to blame for their weight problems. The message of the book is: Sugar makes you fat; only by avoiding it, as well as foods that cause blood sugar to rise, can you lose weight and keep it off. The diet doesn't restrict your total carbohydrate intake, but it forbids or severely restricts the intake of certain carbohydrate foods such as refined sugar, honey, watermelon, rice, pasta, and corn. *SugarBusters!* also includes a little bit of food-combining theory in the mix. For instance, the authors recommend that you eat fruits by themselves, not in combination with other carbohydrates. You don't need to count calories, weigh foods, or calculate grams of carbohydrates on this

This Diet Is Best for: Anyone who wants to cut back on their intake of processed foods and eat more phyto-nutrient-rich plant foods

Who Should Not Try This Diet: No one, although if you exercise heavily it might not provide enough quick energy from simple carbohydrates. Anyone with diabetes whose diet has been very different from *Sugar-Busters!* should check with their doctor first.

plan, but you are expected to balance the portions on your plate and "eyeball" your portion sizes. Not only does the diet promise to help you lose weight, it also says it can help control diabetes and prevent heart disease.

The Rationale

Some experts believe that much of the country's problems with weight stem from the fact that we eat too many sugary foods. Too much sugar, they say, causes the body to overproduce insulin, a hormone that regulates blood sugar levels and fat storage. It's not the excess calories we eat that are the problem, they say, it's the types of foods we eat and how we eat them. The authors of the *SugarBusters!* diet go so far as to claim that fats are not necessarily the cause of weight gain. The theory is that by balancing the

insulin-glucagon relationship in the body (insulin is a hormone that lowers blood sugar when it gets too high, and glucagon is a hormone that raises blood sugar when it goes too low), you'll lose body fat regardless of your calorie intake. In fact, the book says that "most of our body fat comes from ingested sugar, not fat."

Calorie Quota

Calories aren't counted. But if you follow the diet, your calorie intake will be low and you'll lose weight while shifting to a more healthful eating plan.

What's for Breakfast, Lunch, and Dinner?

The *SugarBusters!* diet is based on low glycemic-index carbohydrates (those that have the least effect on blood sugar levels), including high-fiber fruits, vegetables, and whole grains; lean meats; and fats. The book has several charts showing the glycemic index of foods, as well as lists of acceptable foods and foods to avoid. The lower a food's glycemic index, the less effect it has on blood sugar levels and the better it is for weight loss, according to the *SugarBusters!* theory. The book provides two weeks of sample menus; about a quarter of the book is devoted to recipes. Although you don't have to closely track carbohydrate intake, by avoiding refined sugar and processed grains, you'll likely eat far fewer carbohydrates than you do now.

Fact or Fiction: What the Experts Say

This is an area of controversy. Proponents of the insulin theory say that eating a diet full of high glycemic-index foods causes the body to over-produce insulin, prevents the breakdown of fat, and encour-

> ## Quick Take
>
> - Based on the belief that foods with high glycemic indexes stimulate the overproduction of insulin, which results in excess fat storage
> - Recommends lots of unprocessed, whole foods
> - Eliminates sugar and foods high in sugar

ages fat storage. Opponents believe that obesity causes insulin resistance, in which larger and larger amounts of insulin are pumped into the blood in an effort to lower blood sugar. Insulin-theory proponents, on the other hand, say that overproduction of insulin is the cause, rather than the effect, of weight gain. There's research to back up both points of view. Still, most experts are sticking with the current opinion that obesity aggravates insulin production, not the other way around. According to Hope Warshaw, MSc., R.D., a certified diabetes educator and author of *Diabetes and Meal Planning Made Easy*, eating too much of any kind of carbohydrate can cause too much insulin to be produced, and it can result in weight gain

YES-YES'S

Fruits, vegetables, and whole grains

because of the extra calories. The general recommendation today is to tightly control the number of carbohydrate grams you eat rather than worry about the source of those carbohydrates.

NO-NO'S

Sugar and sugar-rich foods, desserts, most processed foods, and all foods with a high glycemic index, including rice, potatoes, beets, carrots, and corn

Gains and Losses/ What's the Damage?

If you set aside some unproven explanations as to why the diet works, *SugarBusters!* offers up a healthful diet plan that encourages eating lots of fruits, vegetables, and whole grains while avoiding junk foods and sweet desserts. Because insulin resistance becomes more common with age and

increases your risk of heart disease, following the diet should help improve your blood sugar regulation and insulin levels as well as reduce your heart disease risk. However, activity is all but dismissed as a waste of time in the battle of the bulge, something that research strongly contradicts. Very little dairy is included in the *Sugar-Busters!* diet plan, so it's likely to be low in calcium and vitamin D—not good for keeping your bones strong as you get older. But a multivitamin plus a calcium supplement should be more than enough to make up the difference.

Other Similar Diets

The Carbohydrate Addict's Lifespan Program

Suzanne Somers' Eat, Cheat, and Melt the Fat Away

The Premise

Somers, who is most famous for her stint on the sitcom *Three's Company* back in the '80s and for her *Thigh Master* infomercials, has also made a successful foray into diet books. This third and latest is little more than an updated edition of her previous book, *Suzanne Somers' Get Skinny on Fabulous Food*. Both diets are based on complex rules of food combining that she developed herself and which she promises will make your body burn fat faster, balance your out-of-whack hormones, and help keep your metabolism set on high. She says her diet is especially helpful for

people over 40, since their metabolism is slower and controlling weight becomes more difficult.

The Rationale

The secret to weight-loss success, healthful aging, and permanent weight loss, says Somers, is proper food combining. The diet has two levels. By following the first level, Somers contends you get rid of diseases such as asthma and irritable bowel syndrome, keep age-related diseases at bay, and lose weight.

She gives "Seven Easy Steps to Somersizing," which are rules about food combining. These are some examples: Eat fruit by itself, eat protein foods and fats with vegetables but not with carbohydrates, eat carbohydrates with vegetables and wait at least three hours between meals when making the switch from protein/fat meals to carbohydrate meals and vice versa. The first level also calls for eliminating all "funky foods," such as sugar, white flour, potatoes, sweet potatoes, bananas, corn, pasta made from semolina or white flour, white rice, low fat and whole milk, and caffeinated and alcoholic beverages.

Level Two of the program focuses on maintaining weight loss. At this point, Somers says you can "cheat" with small amounts of some of the "funky foods." But she doesn't specify how much you can have. And even when you cheat, you must follow her food-combining rules.

Calorie Quota

Calories aren't emphasized in this diet. Because most high-calorie foods are kept to a minimum, chances are that your calorie intake will be low, making it possible for you to lose weight.

This Diet Is Best for: People who don't mind following a set of sometimes arbitrary diet rules that dictate how you can combine your foods and when

Who Should Not Try This Diet: People who have high cholesterol or a history of heart disease and those who eat on the run or eat out a lot

What's for Breakfast, Lunch, and Dinner?

While there are lots of do's and don'ts in Somers' diet, it basically calls for a high-protein, high fat diet in the weight-loss phase. The main "don'ts" include foods that are overly processed and all types of sugar. Carbohydrate-rich foods are limited enough to make the diet low in fiber. She categorizes dairy products together with the non-nutritious "funky foods." The book has 100+ recipes but only one week of sample menus. A typical day's menu might include a fruit smoothie, whole-wheat toast with nonfat cottage cheese, and decaf coffee for breakfast; grilled shrimp and Caesar salad with grilled chicken for lunch; and pork chops with cream sauce, steamed asparagus, and green salad and balsamic vinaigrette dressing for dinner. Two snacks are allowed—an apple and a hard-boiled egg.

Fact or Fiction: What the Experts Say

Although Somers believes that food combining is the key to weight loss, experts say it just isn't so. "She can talk about how calories don't count until the next millennium," says Susan Male Smith, M.A., R.D., editor of *Environmental Nutrition* newsletter. "But the fact is, they do count and there's no magic combination of foods that will alter that fact." There is no solid evidence that combining particular foods at a meal has any sort of weight-loss

---

Quick Take

- Based on unique food-combining principles developed by Suzanne Somers

- Makes almost all dairy foods off-limits

- Limits foods high in starch and sugar and restricts or eliminates high glycemic-index foods

benefit over simply eating a balanced diet.

One of the diet is too high in saturated fat and cholesterol, but it's also high in fruits and vegetables, which is healthy.

YES-YES'S

Foods that rank low on the glycemic-index scale (those that raise blood sugar the least), such as soy, green vegetables, dried beans, fruit, and whole-grain cereals. You may eat rich meats, butter sauces, cheese, eggs, and sour cream but also plenty of fruit and vegetables.

NO-NO'S

Overly processed foods, sugar, foods high in starch, food combinations not prescribed by the plan

Gains and Losses/ What's the Damage?

Since the diet is low in fiber, it could make you constipated. And because Somers allows only one serving of fat-free dairy a day, getting enough calcium and vitamin D in your diet without supplementation could be tough. The diet could be high in saturated fat and cholesterol, depending on which foods you choose. Level

Chances are that if you stick with the diet plan, it will result in weight loss because, despite allowing some high fat foods, it is ultimately low in calories. Somers devotes only five paragraphs to exercise, even though experts agree that losing weight and keeping it off requires regular physical activity, especially for those over 50.

Other Similar Diets

Suzanne Somers' Get Skinny on Fabulous Food, Marilu Henner's Total Health Makeover

STICK-TO-IT-ABILITY RATING: 1 2 **3** 4 5

TOPS (Take Off Pounds Sensibly)

The Premise

TOPS, which stands for Take Off Pounds Sensibly, is a no-frills, low-cost diet plan. Actually, it's not a diet at all but rather a loosely knit support system for people trying to lose weight. Founded in Milwaukee more than 50 years ago, the nonprofit organization has none of the traditional diet plan offerings: There's no official diet, no prepackaged foods, no supplements, and no counseling. But for $20 a year plus local chapter dues of about $5 a month, members can attend weekly support meetings at one of about 9,000 local TOPS chapters (there are 235,000 members), where they will weigh themselves, discuss problems, and even exchange recipes. Chapter leaders are volunteers from the TOPS membership. In addition to weekly support meetings, the national organization offers incentives for weight loss. Once you become a member, you'll receive *TOPS News*, a monthly magazine that offers contests, weight-loss incentive plans, self-help articles, and recipes. TOPS members who reach their goal weight, which is supposed to be set with the help of a health care professional when you join, are eligible for maintenance membership in KOPS (Keep Off Pounds Sensibly). Though TOPS membership is generally comprised of older

> *This Diet Is Best for:* People who prefer to go solo while still having a support group to fall back on
>
> *Who Should Not Try This Diet:* Dieters who know from experience that they need more clear-cut menus and day-to-day guidance on what they should eat and how they should change their eating behaviors

adults, kids and teens are welcome, too.

TOPS now has online help, too, at www.tops.org. In the free portion of the site, you can find most of the material from *TOPS News* and read TOPS success stories. The Web site also has a section called TOPSinteractive, where for a fee you can access chat rooms, forums, and diet and exercise programs.

The Rationale

For people who feel more comfortable figuring out their own path to weight loss, TOPS offers a loose system of support but little more. Exactly what kind of support you'll get from your local chapter is impossible to predict, since chapters vary quite a bit from one to another. In fact, the organization prides itself on the individuality of its chapters. TOPS weekly meetings always begin with a confidential weigh-in, which is followed by a program that sometimes includes presentations by health professionals

Calorie Quota

There is no calorie quota provided, though the optional booklet TOPS offers gives guidance for 1,200-, 1,500-, and 1,800-calorie-a-day diets, using standard food exchange lists.

who volunteer their time to speak. Through group support and some weight-loss competitions, TOPS provides incentives for weight loss. There are national contests as well as local chapter contests. Participants compete only within their own age category and weight class.

Quick Take

- Offers a loosely knit support system of TOPS chapters

- Meetings vary from chapter to chapter throughout the country

- Provides no official diet plan

- Lets dieters develop the approach that works best for them

Choice Is Yours, which contains simple guidelines for planning diets of 1,200, 1,500, and 1,800 calories a day, based on the USDA Food Guide Pyramid and the diabetic exchange list, and it offers a sample 28-day menu and exercise guide.

What's for Breakfast, Lunch, and Dinner?

Because there is no official diet plan or even preset calorie intakes, there are no typical meals. TOPS recommends that its members go to a health care professional for personalized diet and physical activity plans. In addition, the organization does offer an optional diet planning book called *The*

Fact or Fiction: What the Experts Say

Because there is no single TOPS program or diet plan, experts say it's hard to make any kind of judgment as to its safety or effectiveness. However, there's nothing to indicate that the program is unsafe, and for some people, it could be helpful. Just keep in mind that there is no counseling offered and group leaders are untrained volunteers who are also TOPS members.

Gains or Losses/ What's the Damage?

With no set TOPS diet and everyone pretty much on their own in planning their diets, it's hard to say how much you might lose or how quickly you can expect to lose it. Neither the TOPS organization nor the individual chapters make any claims about an expected rate of weight loss. The organization leaves this up to the discretion of each dieter and his or her physician. While this freedom may work well for some people, it carries some risks as well. It could lead some ill-informed dieters to unwittingly cut back too far on calories or to follow an unbalanced diet. However, if you stick with the sample plan provided in TOPS's *The Choice Is Yours* booklet, you should meet most of your nutrient needs while lowering blood cholesterol and controlling blood sugar. It's still a good idea, however, to take a calcium and vitamin D supplement, since it's tough to include enough calcium-rich dairy foods in a 1,200- or 1,500-calorie diet. Though physical activity is recommended and some local chapters incorporate group walks into their weekly meetings, exercise could be emphasized more.

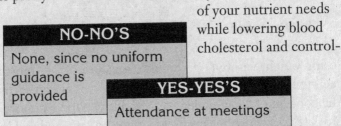

NO-NO'S

None, since no uniform guidance is provided

YES-YES'S

Attendance at meetings

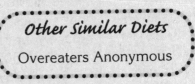

Other Similar Diets

Overeaters Anonymous

Volumetrics

The Premise

This diet is all about losing weight without feeling hungry. It's based on the concept of "energy density," (E.D.) which means how concentrated the calories are in a portion of food. High-energy-density foods provide a large number of calories in a small serving, while low-energy-density foods provide a small number of calories in a large serving. Authors Barbara Rolls, Ph.D., a nutrition researcher at Pennsylvania State University, and journalist Robert Barnett maintain that if you eat mostly low-energy-density foods you can eat more, satisfy your hunger, and still lose weight. For example, you can eat three Chips Ahoy! chocolate chip cookies (53 calories each) or, for the same 160 calories, you can eat 1½ bananas or two apples. The fruit will satisfy you more because it's high in fiber. Fiber and water both fill you up, while water dilutes calories per portion. The higher the water content and/or the

> ### Calorie Quota
> Calories aren't really counted, but the dieter is expected to keep track of the E.D.'s of different foods and stick, as much as possible, with those at the low end of the E.D. scale. However, the diet does suggest that you can reduce your calorie intake by about 500 to 1,000 calories a day by following the diet's guidelines for eating.

higher the fiber content, the lower the energy density of the food and the more volume the food has, which affects how full you feel. Keep fiber intake high, drink a lot of water, and eat a lot of foods high in water content and low in energy density and you will lose weight, promise the authors.

The Rationale

According to the authors' research, we all tend to eat the same average weight in food every day, no matter how many calories the food contains. The Volumetrics approach is to eat the same volume of food but lower the number of calories by eating foods that are higher in fiber and water. If you do, you'll consume fewer calories and lose weight without that empty feeling in your gut. Once you learn to think about the energy density of foods, you'll be surprised by how much food you can eat. While Volumetrics may seem like a gimmick, it's really the same message nutritionists have been preaching for years: Eat more fruits, vegetables, whole grains, legumes, and beans, and eat less high fat, low-nutrient junk foods.

What's for Breakfast, Lunch, and Dinner?

There are no menus that you have to follow and no man-

This Diet Is Best for: People who want some freedom of choice in planning their meals and feel they can go it alone. It is also a good choice for dieters who find it difficult to face an almost empty dinner plate.

Who Should Not Try This Diet: Those who need a step-by-step diet plan and those who need a support system for success

dates as to how or when certain foods should be eaten. Instead, *Volumetrics* contains extensive charts of the energy density (E.D.) and caloric content of one serving of dozens of foods, making it easy to make good low-cal, low-density choices. Though the charts are extensive, you can calculate the E.D. of any food by dividing the number of calories per serving by the weight in grams per serving. Both numbers are usually provided on a product's Nutrition Facts label. The authors provide a collection of 12 breakfast menus, 10 lunch menus, and 25 dinner menus, plus a list of 200-calorie snacks. You'll also find more than 60 pages of recipes for dishes that have low E.D.s. Soup is promoted as an

---

Quick Take

- A diet based on the energy density of foods
- Allows large servings of low-density foods
- Encourages drinking lots of water and eating foods that have a high water content

---

appetite controller, and research is cited showing that eating soup before meals may help control calorie intake due to its high volume, high water content, and low calorie count.

Overall, the diet provides about 20 to 30 percent of calories from fat, 55 percent from carbohydrate, and 15 percent from protein. The diet also includes 20 to 30 grams of fiber a day and lots of water—9 cups a day for women and 12 cups a day for men—from food and beverages.

Fact or Fiction: What the Experts Say

Rolls is an expert in appetite and appetite control and has been researching the topic for years. She has published dozens of scientific papers on the topic and has translated them into a practical diet. According to Liz Ward, M.S., R.D., nutrition counselor in Reading, Massachusetts, "*Volu-*

YES-YES'S

Lots of water, high-fiber foods, fruits and vegetables, large volumes of low-energy-density foods

NO-NO'S

Foods that provide a lot of calories in small servings, restricting total food intake

metrics is all about a dieting philosophy that nutritionists have been preaching for years—choose foods wisely and you can eat more." The authors also make exercise an integral part of the Volumetrics plan, a recommendation about which all experts agree.

Volumetrics formula for eating, you should feel satisfied and still lose weight. Though the plan emphasizes foods with low caloric density, those same foods are high in nutrient density, a real plus for you now that you're over 50. As is the case with even the most well-balanced diets, calcium and vitamin D may still be a concern, and it's best to get nutrition insurance with a calcium and vitamin D supplement to give your bones full protection. The diet also emphasizes fluid intake. While the intent is to fill you up so you don't get hungry, fluid intake is especially important as you get older to avoid dehydration.

Gains and Losses/ What's the Damage?

The diet is a healthful one that encourages the consumption of more plant foods. If you are true to the

Other Similar Diets

The Picture Perfect Diet, The Pritikin Principle

DIETS AT A GLANCE

DIET			
The Age-Free Zone	*Dr. Atkins' Age-Defying Diet Revolution*	*The Carbohydrate Addict's Lifespan Program*	*Choose to Lose*
DIET TYPE			
High-protein, low-calorie, low-carbohydrate	High-protein, low-carbohydrate, antioxidant-rich	High-protein, low-carbohydrate	Balanced, reduced-calorie
MENU			
Protein at each meal and snack, limited complex carbs, no sugars, healthy fats (olive oil) and fatty foods (avocado)	High-protein, high fat foods; no sugars. For weight loss, no more than 60 grams of carbohydrate a day.	Mostly high-protein and low-carbohydrate foods	A variety of foods—lots of fruits, vegetables, lentils, whole grains, olive oil
CALORIES			
Women: about 1,200 calories a day; men: about 1,500 calories a day	No calorie counts	Calories aren't counted, but proportions of foods at meals are controlled	1,500-1,600 per day
NUTRITIONALLY BALANCED			
No. Too high in protein and too low in complex carbohydrates and fiber	No	No	Yes
RISKS			
May be too low in carbohydrates for people with diabetes	Heart disease, possible calcium and vitamin D deficiency	High cholesterol, low blood sugar levels. Low in calcium and fiber.	No risks
STICK-TO-IT-ABILITY RATING			
2	1	2	5

DIETS AT A GLANCE

DIET			
Dieting With the Duchess	*Eat, Drink, and Be Healthy*	*Eat More, Weigh Less*	*Eat Right 4 Your Type*
DIET TYPE			
Balanced, reduced-calorie	Mostly plant-based diet with little dairy	Very low fat (10% of calories), plant-based diet	Varies greatly, depending on blood type
MENU			
Lean meats, lots of fruits and vegetables, fat-free dairy products, lots of water and high-fiber foods	Lots of plant foods—fruits, vegetables, whole grain, legumes. Diary products not essential.	Lots of fruits, vegetables, and whole grains; no oils, sugars, sweeteners, or refined grains	Varies greatly, depending on blood type
CALORIES			
No calorie counts; uses the Weight Watchers point system	Sample menus provide 2,000 calories a day; adjustments given for 1,600 calories	There are no calorie counts, food exchanges, or allowances	No limit on calorie intake
NUTRITIONALLY BALANCED			
Yes	Yes. Could be low in calcium and vitamin D	Yes. Could be low in some essential fatty acids	Food choices are restricted and could be low in some nutrients
RISKS			
No risks	No risks	No risks	Can be nutritionally inadequate
STICK-TO-IT-ABILITY RATING			
4	4	1	1

DIETS AT A GLANCE

DIET			
Eat Right, Live Longer	*Eating Well for Optimum Health*	*Fight Fat Over Forty*	*Fit for Life*
DIET TYPE			
A low fat , high-fiber, vegetarian diet	Mostly plant-based, high-carbohydrate, low fat	Well-balanced, reduced-calorie	Food combining
MENU			
Lots of fruits, vegetables, whole grains, legumes, and healthy fats. No dairy or meat.	Lots of fruits and vegetables, soy foods and those rich in omega-3 fatty acids; little dairy, eggs, meat; plenty of fluids.	Whole grains, fruits, vegetables, nonfat dairy, lean meats, reduced-fat cheeses, foods with a low glycemic index	Fruits, fruit juice in A.M.; mostly fruits, vegetables, and starches in P.M.
CALORIES			
Recommends a minimum of 10 calories per pound of ideal body weight	No calorie counts or specific meal plans	Calories not the focus but plan provides about 1,500 calories a day	No limit on calorie intake
NUTRITIONALLY BALANCED			
Yes, although calcium and vitamin D could be low due to the lack of dairy	Yes	Yes	No
RISKS			
No risks, but could be deficient in calcium and vitamin D	No risks	No risks	Low in calcium, zinc, iron, vitamins B_{12} and D; diarrhea.
STICK-TO-IT-ABILITY RATING			
2	4	4	1

DIETS AT A GLANCE

Jenny Craig	Low-Fat Lies, High-Fat Frauds	Making the Case for Yourself	The Metabolic Typing Diet
DIET TYPE			
Prepackaged diet foods	Mediterranean-style	Reduced food intake made possible by eating smart	Complicated system of eating according to 3 metabolic types
MENU			
Variety of prepackaged entrees, desserts, and snacks; fruits; low fat dairy; whole grains; and vegetables	Fruits, vegetables, whole grains, fish, beans, legumes, olive oil, red wine	Whatever you want—just less of it	Varies greatly depending on metabolic type; proportions of carbs, fats, and protein prescribed by type
CALORIES			
Individualized at 1,000 to 2,300 a day	Guidelines given for 1,500 and 2,000 calories a day	Calories aren't counted	No calorie counts
NUTRITIONALLY BALANCED			
Yes	Yes	No diet plan	The "mixed oxidizer" type appears to be the most balanced of the 3 types
RISKS			
Relapsing when prepackaged food is gradually stopped	For people with alcohol problems	No risks	Two of the types could be low in calcium and vitamin D
STICK-TO-IT-ABILITY RATING			
3	4	5	1

DIETS AT A GLANCE

DIET			
The 90/10 Weight-Loss Plan	*Nutri/System*	*The Okinawa Program*	*The Origin Diet*
DIET TYPE			
Low-calorie; allows a daily 250-calorie "splurge"	Prepackaged diet foods	Low-calorie, high-fiber, high-carbohydrate, antioxidant-rich	Based on the dietary habits of our Stone-Age ancestors
MENU			
A variety of basic foods, plus a lengthy list of 250-calorie foods to splurge on	Prepackaged entrees, desserts, and snacks with added fruits, vegetables, and dairy	Whole grains, vegetables, fruits, foods rich in omega-3 fatty acids and phytonutrients, soy foods	Natural, unprocessed foods and healthy fats like olive and canola oil. No specific diet plan.
CALORIES			
1,200-, 1,400-, and 1,600-calorie-a-day plans	Averages 1,200 calories a day for women and 1,500 for men	There are no calorie counts, just dietary guidelines	Calorie counts are not emphasized—the focus is more on the types of foods eaten
NUTRITIONALLY BALANCED			
Yes, on the higher-calorie plan	Yes	Yes	Yes
RISKS			
Could be low in several nutrients on the 1,200 calorie plan	Relapsing when prepackaged food is gradually stopped	No risks	No risks
STICK-TO-IT-ABILITY RATING			
4	3	2	3

DIETS AT A GLANCE

DIET			
Overeaters Anonymous	*Suzanne Somers' Eat, Cheat, and Melt the Fat Away*	*The RealAge Diet*	*Richard Simmons*
DIET TYPE			
Support group for compulsive overeaters	Food combining	Reduced-fat, reduced-calorie, mainly plant-based	Balanced, reduced-calorie
MENU			
There is no diet plan	Low glycemic-index foods, such as soy, vegetables, fruit, and whole-grain cereals; small amounts of high fat foods	Lots of fruits, vegetables, whole grains, legumes, and soy foods; allows for an occasional treat or glass of wine	Unprocessed foods, fruits, vegetables, whole grains, water
CALORIES			
There are no calorie counts	Calories aren't counted, neither are fat grams or carbohydrates	No emphasis on counting calories	Minimum of 1,200 calories a day
NUTRITIONALLY BALANCED			
n/a	Depends on your food choices	Yes	Yes
RISKS			
Underlying problems not addressed and could get worse	Depends on your food choices	No risks	No risks
STICK-TO-IT-ABILITY RATING			
2	1	4	5

DIETS AT A GLANCE

The Schwarzbein Principle	Dr. Shapiro's Picture Perfect Weight Loss	Slim·Fast	SugarBusters!
DIET TYPE			
High-protein, high fat, low-carbohydrate	Low calorie concentration, high volume	Liquid diet	Low-sugar
MENU			
High-protein, high fat foods; limited whole grains and starchy vegetables; no refined carbohydrates	Anything is allowed as long as calories are controlled	Two liquid meal replacements and one regular meal each day	Foods with low glycemic indexes
CALORIES			
No calorie counts	There is no set calorie count	1,200 or 1,500 calories a day	Calories aren't counted
NUTRITIONALLY BALANCED			
No. Falls short on calcium, vitamin D, folic acid, and fiber	No	No	Yes
RISKS			
Heart disease; possible calcium and vitamin D deficiencies	Could result in low nutrient intakes	Constipation, low in phytochemicals found in fruits and vegetables	Only for people who exercise heavily
STICK-TO-IT-ABILITY RATING			
2	2	2	4

DIETS AT A GLANCE	
DIET	
TOPS	*Volumetrics*
DIET TYPE	
There is no official diet	Reduced-calorie, large volume
MENU	
A reduced-calorie plan, based on food exchanges from all the food groups	Foods with low energy density, water
CALORIES	
Offers 1,200-, 1,500-, and 1,800-calorie-a-day plans	No calorie counts
NUTRITIONALLY BALANCED	
Yes	Yes
RISKS	
No risks	No risks
STICK-TO-IT-ABILITY RATING	
3	5

Resources

Organizations

American Dietetic Association
www.eatright.org
(800) 366-1655
Call or log on to find a dietitian near you. On the Web site you'll find nutrition fact sheets, nutrition tips, and consumer resources.

Tufts University Nutrition Navigator
www.navigator.tufts.edu
This is your gateway to health and nutrition information. Over 200 nutrition links to sites that have been screened for accuracy.

The LEARN Education Center
P.O. Box 610430, Department 70
Dallas, TX 75261-0430
(800) 736-7323
www.learneducation.com
A program of weight management that focuses on lifestyle changes and behavior modification.

Weight-control Information Network (WIN)
1 WIN Way
Bethesda, MD 20892-3665
(301) 984-7378 or
(800) WIN-8098
Fax: (301) 984-7196
www.niddk.nih.gov/health/nutrit/win.htm

Web Sites

www.aboutproduce.com
Everything you always wanted to know about fruits, vegetables, herbs, and nuts, including growing season information, nutrient content, and recipes.

www.cyberdiet.com
Offers advice, support, and nutrition information for dieters.

www.diabeticcooking.com
This site allows you to search hundreds of recipes for people with diabetes. The recipes come with a nutritional breakdown.

www.ediets.com
A subscription-based, full-service, online dieting program that offers personal support, menus, and recipes.

www.fitnessfind.com
Provides information on fitness topics ranging from motivation to weight training.

www.justmove.org
Information on how to get and stay active. Sponsored by the American Heart Association.

www.5aday.nci.nih.gov
National Cancer Institute Web site that offers information about how to eat and exercise to reduce your risk of cancer.

www.mayoclinic.com/findinformation/healthylivingcenter/index.cfm
The Food and Nutrition section of the Healthy Living Center on the Mayo Clinic site has an extensive weight management area. It also provides lots of basic information and recipes developed by the Mayo Clinic's registered dietitians.

www.nal.usda.gov/fnic.com
The USDA Food and Nutrition Information Center contains more than 1,800 links to current and reliable nutrition information as well as a wealth of information about dietary guidelines, supplements, and other nutrition-related consumer issues.

www.nomeat.com
The place to find vegetarian menu items via mail order. Also has recipes and tips for aspiring vegetarians.

www.nutrition.gov
The Food and Drug Administration's site for dieting and nutrition information.

www.soytalk.com
Answers to all your questions about soy and health.

www.weightdirectory.com
This site offers links to more than two dozen other sites related to weight loss, including forums, chat rooms, and exercise guides.